MARCO

FRE

CW00349745

with Local Tips

CONTENTS

CONTENTS

Cover photo: IFA Bilderteam / Förster, Munich
p. 66, 67: Ali Mitgutsch "Let's go to the Sea", "All around my town"
© Ravensburger Buchverlag Otto Maier GmbH

1st English edition 1996 © Mairs Geographischer Verlag, Ostfildern Germany
© based on PONS Reisewörterbuch Französisch
Copyright Ernst Klett Verlag für Wissen und Bildung GmbH, Stuttgart 1992
revised by Gérard Hérin †
Editorial: Ernst Klett Verlag für Wissen und Bildung, Stuttgart;
Mairs Geographischer Verlag, Ostfildern; Barbara Pflüger, Stuttgart
Cover design: Thienhaus/Wippermann, Hamburg
Printed in Italy

Pronunciation

For perfect French pronunciation you will need to listen to a French person and copy what they say. The easy pronunciation guide in this book is designed to help you get started. Remember that in normal speech, the stress tends to fall towards the end of a word or phrase. Also bear in mind that the letters listed below have a slightly different sound in French.

j	sounds like the *"s"* in the English word *"measure"*; for example: *Bonjour!* [bonjoor]
r	is a more gutteral sound in French, made at the back of the throat (think of a dog growling)
n, m	sometimes sound more nasal in French, particularly at the end of a word or after a vowel, like the *"n"* in *"song"* Examples: *pardon* [pardon], *rendez-vous* [rondaivoo]
e	the French *"e"* in words like «*le*» and «*de*» is a short sound, similar to the *"er"* in *"butter"*. It is transcribed as *"er"* in this guide.
‿	Where this liaison sign occurs the two words or sounds should be joined together; for example: *plein air* [plan‿air] *("open air").*

The Alphabet

A	[a]	H	[ash]	O	[o]	V	[vai]
B	[bai]	I	[ee]	P	[pai]	W	[dooblervai]
C	[sai]	J	[jee]	Q	[koo]	X	[eeks]
D	[dai]	K	[ka]	R	[air]	Y	[eegrek]
E	[er]	L	[el]	S	[es]	Z	[zed]
F	[ef]	M	[em]	T	[tai]		
G	[jai]	N	[en]	U	[oo]		

Abbreviations

adj	adjective	*Mme*	Mrs (*Madame*)
adv	adverb	*pl*	plural
s.th.	something	*qc*	something (*quelque chose*)
f	female	*qn*	somebody (*quelqu'un*)
s.b.	somebody	*s.t.p.*	please (informal, singular) (*s'il te plaît*)
m	masculine		
M	Mr (*Monsieur*)	*s.v.p.*	please (formal or plural) (*s'il vous plaît*)
Mlle	Miss (*Mademoiselle*)		

Making friends

Yes.	Oui. [wee]
No.	Non. [non]
Please.	*(formal or plural)* S'il vous plaît. [seel voo plai] / *(informal, singular)* S'il te plaît [seel ter plai]
Not at all!	De rien! [der reeyan]
Thank you.	Merci! [mairsee]
Pardon?	Comment? [komon]
Agreed!	D'accord! [dakor]
OK!/Understood!	Entendu! [ontondoo]
Excuse me.	Pardon! [pardon]
I'd like ...	Je voudrais ... [jer voodrai]
Is there ...?/Are there ...?	(Est-ce qu')Il y a ...? [(es_k)eel_eeya]
Help!	Au secours! [o skoor]

Monsieur, Madame, Mademoiselle

It's always more polite to add «*Monsieur*» [mer_syer], «*Madame*» [madam] or «*Mademoiselle*» [madmwazell] when greeting some-one, and after expressions such as «*merci*» [mairsee] (*"thank you"*), «*oui*» [wee] (*"yes"*) or «*non*» [non] (*"no"*). As a rule, you should only add the surname if the person you are addressing is well known to you.

Who?	Qui? [kee]
What?	Quoi? [kwa]
Which?	Lequel/Laquelle/Lesquels/Lesquelles? [ler_kel/la_kel/lai_kel/lai_kel]
Who ... to?	A qui? [akee]
Who?	Qui [kee]
How much?	Combien? [konbeeyan]
How?	Comment? [komon]
Why?	Pourquoi? [poorkwa]
Where?	Où? [oo]
When?	Quand? [kon]
How long?	Combien de temps? [konbeeyand ton]

GREETINGS

GOOD MORNING/AFTERNOON!	**BONJOUR!** [bonjoor]

Good evening!	Bonsoir! [bonswar]
Hello/Hi!	Salut! [saloo]
What's your name?	Comment vous appelez-vous? [komon vooz aplai voo] / Comment tu t'appelles? [komon too tapell] *(see page 7, box "Formalities")*

MY NAME'S ...	**JE M'APPELLE ...** [jer mapell ...]

Pleased to meet you.	Enchanté/e. [onshontai]
May I introduce you?	Puis-je faire les présentations? [pweej fair lai praizontaseeyon]
This is ...	
Mrs X.	Madame X. [madam]
Miss X.	Mademoiselle X. [madmwazell]
Mr X.	Monsieur X. [mer syer]
How are you?	Comment allez-vous? [komont alai voo] Comment vas-tu? [komon va too]
Fine thanks.	Bien, merci. [beeyan mairsee]
And you?	Et vous-même? [ai voo mem] Et toi? [ai twa]

Greetings

You can't go wrong if you use *«Bonjour!»* [bonjoor] to say hello to someone in French. The more colloquial *«Salut!»* [saloo] should only be used with close acquaintances and friends. Young people use this phrase a lot. When you have got to know someone better, then you greet them with a couple of *bises* [beez] (little kisses) on both cheeks. In some areas three *bises* are customary, in Paris four! However, men usually greet each other with a handshake. The next words you'll hear are the inevitable *«Comment allez-vous/vas-tu?»* [komont alai voo/va too] (*"How are you?"*) or the more familiar *«Ça va?»* [sa va] (*"How's it going?"*). But be warned! The person you're talking to doesn't really want to hear about the state of your health, as the expression is used more as a conversation opener.
Reply with *«Ça va (bien, merci)»* [sa va (beeyan mairsee)] (*"Fine, thanks"*).

Where are you from?	D'où êtes-vous? [doo et voo]
	Tu es d'où? [too ai doo]
I'm from ...	Je suis de ... [jer swee der]
How old are you?	Quel âge avez-vous? [kel_aj avai voo]
	Tu as quel âge? [too a kel aj]
I'm 30.	J'ai 30 ans. [jai tronton]

YES, PLEASE — OUI, JE VEUX BIEN [wee jver beeyan]

Could you do me a favour?	Est-ce que je peux vous demander un petit service? [es_kerj per voo dmondai an ptee sairvees]
May I?	Vous permettez? [voo pairmaitai]
Can you help me, please?	Vous pouvez m'aider, s.v.p.? [voo poovai maidai seel voo plai]

THANK YOU — MERCI! [mairsee]

Thank you very much.	Merci beaucoup! [mairsee bokoo]
No thank you.	Non, merci! [non mairsee]
Thank you. The same to you.	Merci, vous de même/vous aussi! [mairsee vood mem/voo osee]
That's very kind of you, thank you.	C'est gentil, merci! [sai jontee mairsee]
With pleasure.	Avec plaisir! [avek plaizeer]
Don't mention it.	Mais, je vous en prie. [mai jvooz_on pree]
You're welcome.	De rien. [der reeyan]

I'M SORRY! — EXCUSEZ-MOI/EXCUSES-MOI! [aikskoozai mwa/aikskooz mwa]

I'm so sorry!	Je suis navré/désolé. [jer swee navrai/daizolai]
What a pity!	Dommage! [domaj]

Formalities

In French there are two ways of addressing someone: *«vous»* [voo] *("you")* is used with *«Monsieur»* ("Mr.") and *«Madame»* ("Mrs") for a more formal greeting while *«tu»* [too] ("you") is more familiar and used with family and friends. In some very traditional circles in France even married couples use the «Vous» form, as do children addressing their parents.

PARDON? | COMMENT? [komon]

I don't understand.	Je ne comprends pas. [jern konpron pa]
Would you repeat that, please?	Vous pouvez répéter, s'il vous plaît? [voo poovai raipaitai seel voo plai]
Would you speak a bit more slowly, please?	Vous pourriez parler un peu plus lentement, s.v.p.? [voo pooreeyai parlai an per ploo lontmon seel voo plai]
I understand.	Je comprends. [jkonpron]
I only speak a bit of ...	Je parle un tout petit peu ... [jparl an too ptee per]
Would you write it down for me, please?	Vous pouvez me l'écrire, s.v.p.? [voo poovaim laikreer seel voo plai]

MAKING A DATE | RENDEZ-VOUS [rondaivoo]

Have you got any plans for tomorrow?	Vous avez/Tu as des projets pour demain? [vooz_avai/too a dai projai poor dman]
Shall we go together?	On y va ensemble? [on_ee va onsonbl]
When shall we meet?	On se voit à quelle heure? [ons vwa a kel_uhr]
I love you!	Je t'aime! [jer taim]
Are you married?	Vous êtes marié/e? [vooz_et mareeyai]
Have you got a boyfriend/ a girlfriend?	Tu as un petit ami/une petite amie? [too a an pteet_amee/oon pteet_amee]
I've been looking forward to seeing you all day.	J'ai attendu ce moment toute la journée. [jai atondoo smomon toot la joornai]
You've got beautiful eyes!	Tu as des yeux magnifiques! [too a daiz_yer manyeefeek]

"Brilliant"

So you're really having a great time on holiday? Well, here are a few phrases to help you "get that feeling across":

chouette	[shwet]	(nice, cute)
extra	[aikstra]	(fantastic, great)
géant/e	[jayon/jayont]	(so good, great)
génial/e	[jaineeyal]	(brilliant, fab)
sensationnel/le	[sonsaseeyonel]	(amazing)
super	[soopair]	(great)
sympa	[sanpa]	(nice)

«Il est vachement sympa!» [eel_ai vashmon sanpa] ("He's a really nice person!")

8

«Le coup de foudre»

[ler koo dfoodr] ... *"struck by lightning"*, a lovely expression for "love at first sight". *«Avoir le coup de foudre pour quelque chose»* [avvar ler koo dfoodr poor kelker shoze] is used when you are really keen on something, *"to be crazy about something"*.

I've fallen in love with you.	Je suis amoureux *(m)*/amoureuse *(f)* de toi. [jer swee amoorer/amoorerz der twa]
I love you, too.	Moi aussi, je t'aime. [mwa osee jer tem]
Your place or mine?	Chez toi ou chez moi? [shaitwa oo shaimwa]
I would like to sleep with you.	J'aimerais coucher avec toi. [jaimrai kooshai avek twa]
I don't want to.	Je ne veux pas. [jern ver pa]
Stop at once!	Arrête tout de suite! [aret tood sweet]
Only with a condom!	D'accord, mais seulement avec préservatif. [dakor mai suhlmon avek praizairvateef]
Do you have a condom?	Tu as des préservatifs? [too a dai praizairvateef]
Can I take you home?	Je vous/te raccompagne? [j_voo/ter rakonpanyer]
Please leave now!	Vas-t-en maintenant, je t'en prie! [vaton mantnon jer ton pree]
Please leave me alone!	Laissez-moi tranquille, je vous en prie! [laisai mwa tronkeel jer voozon pree]
Go away/Get lost!	Tire-toi! [teer twa]

GOODBYE/BYE!	**AU REVOIR!** [o rervwar]
See you soon!	A bientôt! [a beeyanto]
See you later!	A tout à l'heure! [a toot_a luhr]
See you tomorrow!	A demain! [a dman]
Good night!	Bonne nuit! [bon nwee]
Cheerio!	Salut! [saloo]

"Just good friends"

Even though the French have a certain reputation when it comes to matters of the heart, you shouldn't read too much into the situation if someone tells you they have a lot of *«ami(e)s intimes»* [amee anteem] *("intimate friends")*. He or she is simply lucky to have a number of good, close friends. Even a *«rendez-vous»* [rondaivoo] is usually nothing more than a normal meeting, although it can also mean something more, such as *"a date"*.

CONGRATULATIONS!	**FELICITATIONS!** [faileeseetaseeyon]
Happy birthday!	Bon anniversaire! [bon_aneevairsair]
Good luck!	Bonne chance! [bon shons]
Get well soon!	Je vous/Je te souhaite un prompt rétablissement. [jvoo/jter soowet an pron raitableesmon]
Have a nice weekend!	Bon weekend!

WHERE IS ...?

Excuse me, where's ..., please?	Pardon, Mme/Mlle/M., où se trouve ..., s.v.p.? [pardon madam/madmwazell/mer_syer oos troov ... seel voo plai]
I'm sorry, I don't know.	Je suis désolé, je ne sais pas. [jer swee daizolai jern sai pa]
Which is the quickest way to ... ?	Quel est le chemin le plus court pour aller à ...? [kel_ail shman ler ploo koor poor alai a]
How far is it to walk to ...?	..., c'est à combien d'ici, à pied? [... sait_a konbeeyan deesee a peeyai]
It's a long way.	C'est loin [sai lwan]
It's not far.	Ce n'est pas loin. [snai pa lwan]
Go straight on.	Vous allez tout droit. [vooz alai too drwa]
Turn left/right.	Vous prenez à gauche/à droite. [voo prernai a goshe/a drwat]
The first/second street on the left/right.	La première/deuxième rue à gauche/à droite. [la prermeeyair/derzeeyem roo a goshe/a drwat]
Cross ... the bridge. the square. the street.	Vous traversez ... [voo travairsai] le pont. [ler pon] la place. [la plass] la rue. [la roo]
Then ask again.	Une fois là-bas, vous redemanderez. [oon fwa la ba voo rdermondrai]
You can't miss it.	Vous ne pouvez pas vous tromper. [voon poovai pa voo tronpai]
You can take ... the bus. the tram. the tube (the underground).	Vous pouvez prendre ... [voo poovai prondr] le bus. [ler boos] le tram. [ler tram] le métro. [ler maitro]

THE TIME

TIME	L'HEURE [luhr]

What time is it? — Quelle heure est-il? [kel_uhr ait_eel]

It's (exactly/about) ... — Il est (exactement/environ) ... [eel et (egzaktermon/onveeron)]

three o'clock. — trois heures. [trwaz_uhr]

five past three. — trois heures cinq. [trwaz_uhr sank]

ten past three. — trois heures dix. [trwaz_uhr dees]

quarter past three. — trois heures et quart. [trwaz_uhr ai kar]

half past three. — trois heures et demie. [trwaz_uhr ai dmee]

quarter to four. — quatre heures moins le quart. [katr_uhr mwanl kar]

five to four. — quatre heures moins cinq. [katr_uhr mwan sank]

noon/midnight. — midi/minuit. [meedee/meenwee]

What time?/When? — A quelle heure?/Quand? [a kel_uhr/kon]

At one o'clock. — A une heure. [a oon_uhr]

In an hour's time — Dans une heure. [donz_oon_uhr]

Between three and four o'clock. — Entre trois heures et quatre heures. [ontrer trwaz_uhr ai katr_uhr]

How long? — Combien de temps? [konbeeyand ton]

For two hours. — Pendant deux heures. [pondon derz_uhr]

From ten to eleven. — De dix à onze. [der dees a onz]

Till five o'clock. — Jusqu'à/Avant cinq heures. [jooska/avon sank_uhr]

Since when? — Depuis quelle heure? [derpwee kel_uhr]

Since eight a.m. — Depuis huit heures du matin. [derpwee weet_uhr doo matan]

For half an hour. — Depuis une demi-heure. [derpwee oon dermeeyuhr]

AUTRES INDICATIONS DE TEMPS [otrerz_andeekaseeyon der ton]

about noon/midday/lunchtime	vers midi [vair meedee]
at lunchtime	à midi [a meedee]
at night	de nuit [der nwee]
every day	tous les jours [too lai joor]
every half hour	toutes les demi-heures [toot lai dermeeyuhr]
every hour, hourly	par heure [par_uhr]
every other day	tous les deux jours [too lai der joor]
from time to time	de temps en temps [der tonz_on ton]
in a fortnight's time	dans quinze jours [don kanz joor]
in the afternoon	dans l'après-midi [don lapraimeedee]
in the evening	le soir [ler swar]
in the morning	le matin [ler matan]
last Monday	lundi dernier [landee dairneeyai]
next year	l'année prochaine [lanai proshen]
now	maintenant [mantnon]
recently, the other day . . .	l'autre jour [lotrer joor]
sometimes	quelquefois [kelkerfwa]
soon	bientôt [beeyanto]
ten minutes ago	il y a dix minutes [eel_eeya dee meenoot]
the day after tomorrow . . .	après-demain [aprai dman]
the day before yesterday . .	avant-hier [avont_eeyair]
this week	cette semaine [set smen]
today	aujourd'hui [ojoordwee]
tomorrow	demain [dman]
within a week	en une semaine [on oon smen]
yesterday	hier [eeyair]

THE DATE | **LA DATE** [la dat]

What's the date (today)?	On est le combien aujourd'hui? [onn_ail konbeeyan ojoordwee]
Today's the first of May.	Aujourd'hui, c'est le 1er mai. [ojoordwee sail prermeeyai mai]

DAYS OF THE WEEK — LES JOURS DE LA SEMAINE [lai joor der la smen]

Monday	lundi [landee]
Tuesday	mardi [mardee]
Wednesday	mercredi [mairkrerdee]
Thursday	jeudi [juhdee]
Friday	vendredi [vondrerdee]
Saturday	samedi [samdee]
Sunday	dimanche [deemonsh]

MONTHS OF THE YEAR — LES MOIS DE L'ANNEE [lai mwa der lanai]

January	janvier [jonveeyai]	July	juillet [jweeyai]
February	février [faivreeyai]	August	août [oot]
March	mars [mars]	September	septembre [septonbr]
April	avril [avreel]	October	octobre [oktobr]
May	mai [mai]	November	novembre [novonbr]
June	juin [jwan]	December	décembre [daisonbr]

SEASONS — LES SAISONS [lai saizon]

spring	le printemps [ler pranton]	autumn	l'automne m [loton]
summer	l'été m [laitai]	winter	l'hiver m [leevair]

HOLIDAYS — LES JOURS FERIES [lai joor faireeyai]

New Year's Day	le Nouvel An [ler noovel_on]
Epiphany	la Fête des Rois [la fet dai rwa]
	l'Epiphanie [laipeefanee]
Carnival	le carnaval [ler karnaval]
Shrove Tuesday	le mardi gras [ler mardee gra]
Ash Wednesday	le mercredi des cendres [ler mairkrerdee dai sondr]
Good Friday	le vendredi saint [ler vandrerdee san]
Easter	Pâques f [pak]
The May bank holiday	la Fête du Travail [la fet doo travaeey]
Ascension Day	l'Ascension f [lasonseeyon]
Whit-Sunday	la Pentecôte [la pontkot]
Corpus Christi	la Fête-Dieu [la fet deeyer]
July 14th (Bastille Day)	le quatorze juillet [ler katorz jweeyai]
Assumption	l'Assomption f [lasonpseeyon]
All Saints' Day (1. Nov.)	la Toussaint [la toosan]
Armistice Day (11. Nov.)	l'Armistice m [larmeestees]
Christmas Eve	la veille de Noël [la vay der noel]
Christmas	Noël [noel]
New Year's Eve	la Saint-Sylvestre [la san seelvestr]

What's the weather going to be like today?	Qu'est-ce qu'il va faire comme temps, aujourd'hui? [kes_keel va fair kom ton ojoordwee]
It's going to stay fine.	Le temps restera au beau. [ler ton raisterra o bo]
It's going to get warmer/colder.	Le temps va se radoucir/se rafraîchir. [ler ton va ser radooseer/ser rafraisheer]
It's going to rain/snow.	Il va pleuvoir/neiger. [eel va plervwar/naijai]
It's cold/hot/close.	Il fait froid/chaud/lourd. [eel fai frwa/sho/loor]
What's the temperature today?	Quelle température fait-il, aujourd'hui? [kel tonpairatoor fait_eel ojoordwee]
It's 20 °C.	Il fait vingt degrés. [eel fai van dergrai]

air	l'air *m* [lair]
black ice	le verglas [ler vairgla]
changeable	variable [vareeyabl]
climate	le climat [ler kleema]
cloud	le nuage [ler nooaj]
cloudy	nuageux [nooajuhr]
cold	froid [frwa]
dry	sec, sèche [sek, sesh]
flooding, floods	l'inondation *f* [leenondaseeyon]
fog	le brouillard [ler brooeeyar]
frost	le gel [ler jel]
heat	la chaleur [la shaluhr]
high tide	la marée haute [la marai ot]
hot	très chaud [trai sho]
humid	lourd [loor]
lightning	l'éclair *m* [laiklair]
low tide	la marée basse [la marai bas]
rain	la pluie [la plwee]
rainy	pluvieux [plooveeyuhr]
snow	la neige [la naij]
sun	le soleil [ler solay]
sunny	ensoleillé [onsolayai]
temperature	la température [la tonpairatoor]
thunder	le tonnerre [ler tonair]
thunderstorm	l'orage *m* [loraj]
warm	chaud [sho]
wet	humide [oomeed]
wind	le vent [ler von]

How far is it?

... BY CAR/MOTORBIKE/BIKE

EXCUSE ME, HOW DO I GET TO ...?	**POUR ALLER A ..., S'IL VOUS PLAIT?** [poor_alai a seel voo plai]
How far is it?	C'est à combien de kilomètres d'ici? [sait_a konbeeyand keelometr deesee]
Excuse me, is this the road to ...?	Pardon, Mme/Mlle/M., je suis bien sur la route de ...? [pardon madam/ madmwazell/ mer_syer jer swee beeyan soor la root der]
How do I get to the ... motorway?	Pour rejoindre l'autoroute de ..., s.v.p.? [poor rerjwandr lotoroot der ... seel voo plai]
You go straight on until you get to ...	Vous allez tout droit jusqu'à ... [vooz_alai too drwa jooska]
Then turn left/right.	Ensuite, vous tournez à gauche/à droite. [onsweet voo toornai a goshe/a drwat]

FILL HER UP, PLEASE.	**LE PLEIN, S.V.P.** [ler plan seel voo plai]
Where's the nearest petrol station, please?	Pardon, Mme/Mlle/M., où est la station-service la plus proche, s.v.p.? [pardon madam/madmwazell/mer_syer oo ai la staseeyon sairvees la ploo prosh seel voo plai]
I'd like ... litres ...	... litres, s'il vous plaît. [leetr seel voo plai]
three-star.	De l'ordinaire. [der lordeenair]
four-star.	Du super. [doo soopair]
diesel.	Du gas-oil. [doo gazwal]
unleaded/leaded.	Du sans-plomb/... octanes. [doo son plon/ ... oktan]
Please check ...	Vérifiez ..., s.v.p. [vaireefeeyai ... seel voo plai]
the oil.	le niveau d'huile [ler neevo dweel]
the tyre pressure.	la pression des pneus [la praiseeyon dai pner]

15

PARKING — **LE STATIONNEMENT** [ler staseeyonmon]

| Is there a car-park near here? | Pardon, Mme/Mlle/M., est-ce qu'il y a un parking près d'ici, s.v.p.? [pardon madam/madmwazell/mer_syer es_keel_eeya an parkeeng prai deesee seel voo plai] |
| Can I park my car here? | Je peux garer ma voiture ici? [jper garai ma vwatoor_eesee] |

MY CAR'S BROKEN DOWN — **JE SUIS EN PANNE** [jer sweez_on pan]

I've got a flat tyre.	J'ai un pneu crevé. [jai an pner krervai]
Would you send ...	Est-ce que vous pouvez m'envoyer ... [es_ker voo poovai monvwaeeyai]
a mechanic/ a breakdown truck, please?	un mécanicien [an maikaneeseeyan]/ une dépanneuse [oon daipanerz], s.v.p. [seel voo plai]
Could you give me some petrol, please?	Vous pourriez me donner un peu d'essence, s.v.p.? [voo pooreeyaim donai an per daisons seel voo plai]
Could you help me change the tyre, please?	Vous pourriez m'aider à changer la roue, s.v.p. [voo pooreeyai maidai a shonjai la roo seel voo plai]
Could you give me a lift to the nearest garage?	Est-ce que vous pouvez m'emmener jusqu'au prochain garage? [es_ker voo poovai momnai joosko proshan garaj]

IS THERE A GARAGE NEAR HERE? — **EST-CE QU'IL Y A UN GARAGE PRES D'ICI?** [es_keel_eeya an garaj prai deesee]

The car won't start.	Ma voiture ne démarre pas. [ma vwatoor ner daimar pa]
The battery is flat	La batterie est à plat. [la batree ait_a pla]
There's something wrong with the engine.	J'ai des ennuis de moteur. [jai daiz_onnweed motuhr]
The brakes don't work.	Mes freins ne répondent pas bien. [mai fran ner raipond pa beeyan]
... is faulty.	... est défectueux. [... ai daifektooer]
I'm losing oil.	Il y a une fuite d'huile. [eel_eeya oon fweet dweel]
Could you have a look?	Vous pouvez jeter un coup d'œil, s.v.p.? [voo poovai jetai an koo day seel voo plai]
Change the spark-plugs, please.	Changez les bougies, s.v.p. [shonjai lai boojee seel voo plai]
How much will it be?	Ca va me coûter combien? [sa vam kootai konbeeyan]

THERE'S BEEN AN ACCIDENT
IL Y A UN ACCIDENT
[eel_eeya ann_akseedon]

Please call ...	Appelez vite ... [aplai veet]
an ambulance.	une ambulance. [oon_onboolons]
the police.	la police. [la polees]
the fire brigade.	les pompiers. [lai ponpeeyai]
Have you got a first-aid kit?	Vous avez une trousse de secours? [vooz_avai oon troos der skoor]
It was my fault.	C'est moi qui suis en tort. [sai mwa kee sweez_on tor]
It was your fault.	C'est vous qui êtes en tort. [sai voo kee etz_on tor]
Shall we call the police, or can we settle things ourselves?	On appelle la police ou on fait un constat à l'amiable? [onn_apel la polees oo on fai an konsta a lameeyabl]
I'd like my insurance company to take care of the damage.	Je veux faire régulariser le dommage par mon assurance. [jer ver fair raigoolareezai ler domaj par monn_asoorons]
Please give me your name and address/particulars of your insurance company.	Vous pouvez me donner votre nom et votre adresse/le nom et l'adresse de votre compagnie d'assurances. [voo poovai mer donai votr non ai votr_adress/ler non ai ladress der votr konpanyee dasoorons]
Thank you very much for your help.	Je vous remercie beaucoup de votre aide. [jer voo rermairsee bokoo der votr_aid]

CAR/MOTORBIKE/BICYCLE HIRE
LOCATION D'UNE VOITURE/ D'UNE MOTO/D'UN VELO
[lokaseeyon doon vwatoor/doon moto/dan vailo]

I'd like to hire ... for two days/for a week.	Je voudrais louer pour deux jours/ une semaine ... [jvoodrai looai poor der joor/oon smen]
a car	une voiture. [oon vwatoor]
a motorbike	une moto. [oon moto]
a bike	un vélo. [an vailo]
What do you charge per kilometre?	Quel est le prix au km? [kel_ail pree o keelometr]
Does the vehicle have comprehensive insurance?	Est-ce que le véhicule est assuré tous risques? [es_ker ler vai_eekyool ait_asoorai too reesk]
Is it possible to leave the car in ...?	Est-ce qu'il est possible de rendre le véhicule à ...? [es_keel_ai poseebl der rondr ler vai_eekyool a]

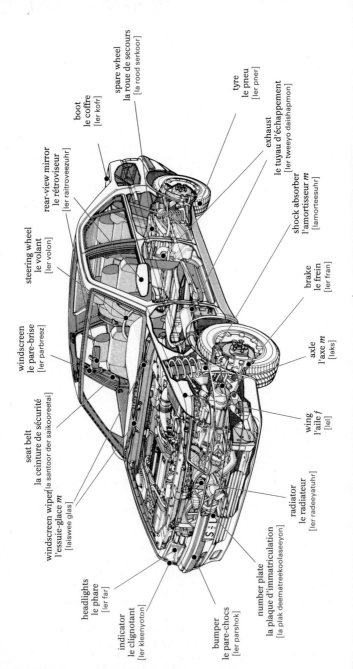

spare wheel
la roue de secours
[la rood serkoor]

tyre
le pneu
[ler pner]

exhaust
le tuyau d'échappement
[ler tweeyo daishapmon]

shock absorber
l'amortisseur *m*
[lamorteesuhr]

brake
le frein
[ler fran]

axle
l'axe *m*
[laks]

wing
l'aile *f*
[lel]

radiator
le radiateur
[ler radeeyatuhr]

number plate
la plaque d'immatriculation
[la plak deematreekoolaseeyon]

bumper
le pare-chocs
[ler parshok]

indicator
le clignotant
[ler kleenyoton]

headlights
le phare
[ler far]

windscreen wiper
l'essuie-glace *m*
[laiswee glas]

seat belt
la ceinture de sécurité
[la santoor der saikooreetai]

windscreen
le pare-brise
[ler parbreez]

steering wheel
le volant
[ler volon]

rear-view mirror
le rétroviseur
[ler raitroveezuhr]

boot
le coffre
[ler kofr]

18

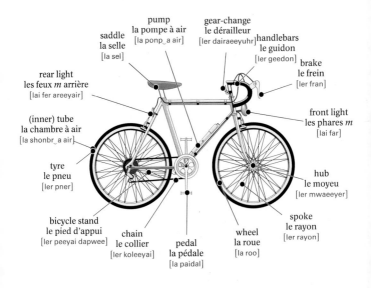

pump
la pompe à air
[la ponp_a air]

gear-change
le dérailleur
[ler dairaeeyuhr]

handlebars
le guidon
[ler geedon]

saddle
la selle
[la sel]

brake
le frein
[ler fran]

rear light
les feux *m* arrière
[lai fer areeyair]

front light
les phares *m*
[lai far]

(inner) tube
la chambre à air
[la shonbr_a air]

tyre
le pneu
[ler pner]

hub
le moyeu
[ler mwaeeyer]

bicycle stand
le pied d'appui
[ler peeyai dapwee]

chain
le collier
[ler koleeyai]

pedal
la pédale
[la paidal]

wheel
la roue
[la roo]

spoke
le rayon
[ler rayon]

accelerator	l'accélérateur *m* [laksailairatuhr]
alcohol level	le taux d'alcoolémie
	[ler tow dalkolaimee]
automatic (transmission)	le changement de vitesse automatique
	[ler shonjmond veetess otomateek]
backfire	l'allumage *m* défectueux
	[laloomaj daifaiktooer]
bell	le timbre [ler tanbr]
bend	le virage [ler veeraj]
bicycle, bike	le vélo [ler vailo]
brake lining	la garniture de frein
	[la garneetoor der fran]
breakdown	la panne [la pan]
breakdown service	le service de dépannage
	[ler sairvees der daipanaj]
breakdown vehicle	la dépanneuse [la daipanerz]
broken	cassé [kasai]
cable	le câble [ler kabl]
car body	la carrosserie [la karosree]
car park	le parking [ler parkeeng]
car wash	le lavage [ler lavaj]
carburettor	le carburateur [ler karbooratuhr]
clutch	l'embrayage *m* [lonbrayaj]
cooling water	l'eau *f* de refroidissement
	[lod rerfrwadeesmon]
country road	la route nationale [la root naseeyonal]
crash helmet	le casque de moto [ler kask der moto]
crossroads	le carrefour [ler karfoor]

dipped headlights	le phare code [ler far kod]
diversion	la déviation [la daiveeyaseeyon]
driving-licence	le permis de conduire
	[ler pairmeed kondweer]
dynamo	la dynamo [la deenamo]
emergency telephone	le téléphone de secours
	[ler tailaifon der skoor]
fan belt	la courroie [la koorwa]
fault	le défaut [ler daifo]
filling station	la station-service [la staseeyonsairvees]
fine	l'amende f [lamond]
flat (tyre)	le pneu à plat [ler pner a pla]
footbrake	la pédale de frein [la paidal der fran]
full-beam	les feux m de route [lai ferd root]
fully comprehensive	(l'assurance f) tous risques
insurance	[(lasoorons) too reesk]
fuse	le fusible [ler foozeebl]
garage	le garage [ler garaj]
gear	la vitesse [la veetess]
gear lever	le levier du changement de vitesses
	[ler lerveeyai doo shonjmond veetess]
gearbox	la boîte de vitesses [la bwat der veetess]
green card	la carte verte [la kart vairt]
handbrake	le frein à main [ler fran a man]
hazard warning light	le signal de détresse
	[ler seenyal der daitress]
heating	le chauffage [ler shofaj]
hitch-hiker	l'auto-stoppeur/l'auto-stoppeuse
	[lotostopuhr/lotostoperz]
horn	le klaxon [ler klakson]
hp (horsepower)	CV, chevaux-vapeurs
	[sai vai, shervo vapuhr]
ignition key	la clé de contact [la klaid kontakt]
ignition	l'allumage m [laloomaj]
jack	la cric [la kreek]

Road Signs

Arrêt interdit	(No stopping)
Attention	(Danger)
Dérapage	(Danger of skidding)
Descente dangereuse	(Steep gradient)
Ecole	(Beware school children)
Priorité à droite	(Give way to the right)
Prudence	(Caution)
Ralentir	(Slow down)
Rappel	(Reminder of a previous warning or prohibitive sign)
Stationnement interdit	(No parking)
Virage dangereux	(Dangerous bend)

jump lead	le câble de démarrage [ler kabl der daimaraj]
lane	la voie [la vwa]
lorry	le camion [ler kameeyon]
motor, engine	le moteur [ler motuhr]
motorbike	la moto [la moto]
motorway	l'autoroute f [lotoroot]
mudguard	le garde-boue [ler gard boo]
multi-storey car park	le parking couvert [ler parkeeng koovair]
octane number	le chiffre d'octane [ler sheefrer doktan]
oil	l'huile f [lweel]
oil change	la vidange [la veedonj]
papers	les papiers m [lai papeeyai]
petrol	l'essence m [laisons]
petrol can	le jerrycan [ler jaireekan]
petrol pump	la pompe à essence [la ponp_a aisons]
petrol station	la station-service [la staseeyonsairvees]
puncture	le pneu à plat [ler pner a pla]
(puncture) repair kit	le nécessaire de réparation des pneus [ler naisaisair der raiparaseeyon dai pner]
radar speed check	le contrôle radar [ler kontrol radar]
rim	la jante [la jont]
road map	la carte routière [la kart rooteeyair]
roadworks	le chantier [ler shonteeyai]
scooter	le scooter [ler skootair]
screw	la vis [la vees]
seal (join)	le joint [ler jwan]
services	l'aire f de repos [lair der rerpo]
short-circuit	le court-circuit [ler koorseerkwee]
sidelights	les feux m de position [lai ferd pozeeseeyon]
sign	le poteau indicateur [ler poto andeekatuhr]
spanner, wrench	la clé anglaise [la klai onglaiz]
spark-plug	la bougie [la boojee]
speedometer	le compteur [ler kontuhr]
starter	le démarreur [ler daimaruhr]
station	la station-service [la staseeyonsairvees]
street, road	la rue [la roo]
sunroof	le toit ouvrant [ler twa oovron]
tools	l'outil m [lootee]
tow-rope	le câble de remorquage [ler kabl der rermorkaj]
traffic jam	l'embouteillage m [lonbootayaj]
traffic lights	le feu (de circulation) [ler fer (der seerkoolaseeyon)]
to tow (away)	remorquer [rermorkai]
valve	la soupape [la soopap]
warning triangle	le triangle de présignalisation [ler treeyongl der praiseenyaleezaseeyon]

TAKE-OFF | LE DEPART [ler daipar]

Where's the ... counter?	Où se trouve le guichet de la compagnie ...? [oos troov ler geeshai der la konpanyee]
When's the next flight to ...?	Quand part le prochain avion pour ...? [kon par ler proshen_aveeyon poor]
I'd like to book a single/return flight to ...	Je voudrais un billet d'avion pour ..., aller simple/aller-retour. [jvoodrai an beeyai daveeyon poor ... alai sanpl/alai rtoor]
Are there still seats available?	Est-ce qu'il y a encore des places de libres? [es_keel_eeya onkor dai plass der leebr]
Non-smoking, please.	Une place non-fumeurs, s'il vous plaît. [oon plass non foomuhr seel voo plai]
I'd like to cancel this flight.	Je voudrais annuler ce vol. [jer voodrai anoolai ser vol]
Can I take this as hand luggage?	Est-ce que je peux prendre cela en bagage à main? [es_kerj per prondr sla on bagaj a man]
Is the plane to ... late?	Est-ce que l'avion pour ... a du retard? [es_ker laveeyon poor ... a du rtar]

ARRIVAL | L'ARRIVEE [lareevai]

My luggage is missing.	Mes bagages ont été égarés. [mai bagaj ont_aitai aigarai]
My suitcase has been damaged.	Ma valise est abîmée. [ma valeez ait_abeemai]

airline	la compagnie aérienne [la konpanyee a_aireeyen]
airport bus	le bus desservant l'aéroport [ler boos daisairvon laairopor]
airport tax	les droits *m* d'aéroport [lai drwa da_airopor]
boarding card	la carte d'embarquement [la kart donbarkmon]
booking	la réservation [la raisairvaseeyon]
to cancel	annuler [anoolai]
captain	le commandant [ler komondon]

22

to change the booking ...	modifier [modeefeeyai]
charter flight	le charter [ler shartair]
to check in	faire les formalités *f* d'embarquement [fair lai formaleetai donbarkmon]
connection	la correspondance [la koraispondons]
counter	le guichet [ler geeshai]
crew	l'équipage *m* [laikeepaj]
delay	le retard [ler rertar]
direct flight	le vol direct [ler vol deerekt]
duty-free shop	le magasin hors-taxe [ler magzan or taks]
emergency chute	le toboggan d'évacuation [ler tobogan daivakooaseeyon]
emergency exit	la sortie de secours [la sortee skoor]
emergency landing	l'atterrissage *m* forcé [lataireesaj forsai]
to fasten one's seat belt ...	attacher sa ceinture [atashai sa santoor]
flight	le vol [ler vol]
(flight) timetable	l'horaire *m* des vols [lorair dai vol]
hand luggage/baggage ...	les bagages *m* à main [lai bagaj a man]
helicopter	l'hélicoptère *m* [laileekoptair]
landing	l'atterrissage *m* [lataireesaj]
life-jacket	le gilet de sauvetage [ler jilaid sovtaj]
luggage	les bagages *m* [lai bagaj]
non-smoking	non-fumeurs [non foomuhr]
on board	à bord (de l'appareil) [a bor (der laparay)]
passenger	le passager *(m)*/la passagère *(f)* [ler pasajai /la pasajair]
pilot	le pilote [ler peelot]
plane	l'avion *m* [laveeyon]
scheduled flight	le vol régulier [ler vol raigooleeyai]
runway	la piste [la peest]
scheduled time of departure	le décollage prévu [ler daikolaj praivoo]
seat belt	la ceinture [la santoor]
security control	le contrôle de sécurité [ler kontrol der saikooreetai]
smoking	fumeurs [foomuhr]
steward/stewardess	le steward/l'hôtesse *f* de l'air [ler steward/lotess der lair]
stopover	l'escale *f* [leskal]
time of arrival	l'heure *f* d'arrivée [luhr dareevai]
window seat	le coin-hublot [ler kwan ooblo]

... BY TRAIN

DEPARTURE | LE DEPART [ler daipar]

When's the next train to ...?

A quelle heure part le prochain train pour ...? [a kel uhr par ler proshan tran poor]

A second-class/first-class single to ..., please.

Un aller deuxième/première classe pour ..., s.v.p. [ann_alai derzeeyem/prermeeyair klas poor ... seel voo plai]

Two returns to ..., please.

Deux aller-retour pour ..., s'il vous plaît. [derz_alai rtoor poor ... seel voo plai]

Is there a reduction for children/students?

Est-ce qu'il y a des réductions pour les enfants/les étudiants? [es_keeleeya dai-raidookseeyon poor laiz_onfon/laiz_aitoodeeyon]

I'd like to reserve a seat on the ... o'clock train to ...

Je voudrais réserver une place dans le train de ... heures pour ... [jvoodrai raizairvai oon plass don ler tran der ... uhr poor]

Is the train from ... running late?

Est-ce que le train de ... a du retard? [es_ker ler tran der ... a doo rtar]

Is there a connection to a ferry at ...?

Est-ce que je peux prendre le ferry-boat à ...? [es_kerj per prondr ler feree bot a]

(Where) Do I have to change?

(Où) Est-ce que je dois changer? [(oo) es_kerj dwa shonjai]

Which platform does the ... train leave from?

Le train pour ... part à quelle voie, s'il vous plaît? [ler tran poor ... par a kel vwa seel voo plai]

ON THE TRAIN | DANS LE TRAIN [don ler tran]

Excuse me, is this seat free?

Pardon, Mme/Mlle/M., est-ce que cette place est libre, s.v.p.? [pardon madam/madmwazell/mer_syer es_ker set plass_ai leebr seel voo plai]

Does this train stop in ...?

Est-ce que le train s'arrête à ...? [es_ker ler tran saret a]

to arrive .... arriver [areevai]
compartment .... le compartiment [ler konparteemon]
departure .... le départ [ler daipar]
emergency brake .... le signal d'alarme [ler seenyal dalarm]
fare .... le prix de la course [ler pree dla koors]
fast train .... le rapide [ler rapeed]
free .... libre [leebr]

24

to get on	monter (dans le train) [montai (donl tran)]
to get out	descendre [daisondr]
half-fare	le demi-tarif [ler dmeetareef]
left-luggage office	la consigne [la konseenyer]
left-luggage ticket	le bulletin de consigne [ler booltand konseenyer]
through train	le train direct [ler tran deerekt]
luggage	les bagages m [lai bagaj]
main station	la gare principale [la gar pranseepal]
motorail service (by night/ day)	le train autos-couchettes/autos-jour [ler tran otokooshet/otojoor]
no-smoking compartment	le compartiment «non-fumeurs» [ler konparteemon non foomuhr]
platform	la voie [la vwa]
railway	le chemin de fer [ler shermand fair]
reduction	la réduction [la raidookseeyon]
reservation	la réservation [la raizairvaseeyon]
restaurant car	le wagon-restaurant [ler vagon raistoron]
return ticket	le billet aller-retour [ler beeyai alai rtoor]
seat reservation	le ticket de réservation [ler teekai der raizairvaseeyon]
smoking compartment ...	le compartiment «fumeurs» [ler konparteemon foomuhr]
station	la gare [la gar]
station restaurant	le buffet de la gare [ler boofaid la gar]
stop	l'arrêt m (en gare) [larai (on gar]]
supplement	le supplément [ler sooplaimon]
taken	occupé [okoopai]
ticket	le billet [ler beeyai]
ticket office	le guichet des billets [ler geeshai dai beeyai]
time of departure	l'heure f de départ [luhr der daipar]
timetable	l'horaire m (de chemin de fer) [lorair (der shermand fair)]
toilet	les toilettes f [lai twalet]
train	le train [ler tran]
vacant	libre [leebr]
waiting-room	la salle d'attente [la sal datont]
window-seat	le coin-fenêtre [ler kwan fnaitr]

... BY BOAT

AT THE PORT	**DANS LE PORT** [don ler por]
When does the next ship leave for ...	A quelle heure part le prochain bateau pour ...? [a kel uhr par ler proshan bato poor ...]

25

How long does the crossing take?	La traversée dure combien de temps? [la travaisai door konbeeyand ton]
When do we land at ...?	Quand est-ce qu'on arrive à ...? [kont_es konn_areev a]
I'd like a ticket to ...	Je voudrais un billet pour ... [jvoodrai an beeyai poor]
I'd like a ticket for the ... o'clock departure.	Je voudrais un billet pour le départ de ... heures. [jvoodrai an beeyai poor ler daipar der ... uhr]

ON BOARD	À BORD [a bor]
Where's the restaurant/lounge?	Où est la salle à manger/le salon? [oo ai la sal_a monjai/ler salon]
I don't feel well.	Je ne me sens pas très bien. [jern mer son pa trai beeyan]
Could you give me something for seasickness, please.	Donnez-moi un médicament contre le mal de mer, s.v.p. [donai mwa an maideekamon kontrer ler mal der mair seel voo plai]

booking	la réservation [la raisairvaseeyon]
cabin	la cabine [la kabeen]
captain	le commandant [ler komondon]
coast	la côte [la kot]
deck	le pont [ler pon]
dock	l'embarcadère *m* [lonbarkadair]
ferry	*(car)* le bac [ler bak]
	(train) le ferry-boat [ler fereebot]
hovercraft	l'hovercraft *m* [lovuhrkraft]
lifebelt	la bouée de sauvetage [la booaid sovtaj]
lifeboat	le canot de sauvetage [ler kanod sovtaj]
life-jacket	le gilet de sauvetage [ler jeelaid sovtaj]
mainland, dry land	la terre ferme [la tair fairm]
motorboat	le canot automobile [ler kano otomobeel]
on board	à bord [a bor]
passenger	le passager *(m)*/la passagère *(f)* [ler pasajai /la pasajair]
port	le port [ler por]
rough seas	la mer agitée [la mair ajitai]
rowing-boat	la barque (à rames) [la bark (a ram)]
seasick, to be ~	avoir le mal de mer [avvar ler mal der mair]
steamer, steamship	bateau à vapeur [bato a vapuhr]
steward	le steward [ler steevward]
ticket	le billet [ler beeyai]

What to see and where to go

I'd like a map of the town.	Je voudrais un plan de la ville. [jvoodrai an plon der la veel]
What places of interest are there here?	Quelles sont les curiosités de la ville? [kel son lai kooreeyozeetaid la veel]
Are there sightseeing tours of the city?	Est-ce qu'il y a des tours de ville organisés? [es_keel_eeya dai toor der veel organeezai]
How much does the tour cost?	Quel est le prix du billet? [kel_ail pree doo beeyai]
Are we going to see ..., too?	Est-ce qu'on va visiter également ...? [es_kon va veezeetai aigalmon]
When are we going back?	A quelle heure est-ce que nous repartons? [a kel_uhr es_ker noo rparton]

SIGHTS

When's the museum open?	A quelle heure ouvre le musée? [a kel_uhr oovrer ler moozai]
When does the tour start?	La visite guidée est à quelle heure? [la veezeet geedai ait_a kel_uhr]
Is this (that) ...?	C'est ..., ça? [sai ... sa]

altar	l'autel *m* [lotell]
architecture	l'architecture *f* [larsheetektoor]
building	le bâtiment [ler bateemon]
castle	le château [ler shato]
cathedral	la cathédrale [la kataidral]
cemetery	le cimetière [ler seemteeyair]
chapel	la chapelle [la shapell]
church	l'église *f* [laigleez]
city centre, town centre . .	le centre-ville [ler sontr veel]
covered market	les halles [lai al]

27

day trip	l'excursion *f* pour une journée [lekskoorseeyon poor oon joornai]
emperor	l'empereur [lonpruhr]
empress	l'impératrice [lanpairatreess]
excavations	les fouilles *f* [lai fooeey]
excursion, trip	l'excursion *f* [lekskoorseeyon]
exhibition	l'exposition *f* [lekspozeeseeyon]
fishing port	le port de pêche [ler por der pesh]
fortress, castle	la forteresse [la forterress]
gallery	la galerie [la galerree]
guide	le guide [ler geed]
guided tour	la visite guidée [la veezeet geedai]
king	le roi [ler rwa]
lake	le lac [ler lak]
market	le marché [ler marshai]
monument	le monument [ler monoomon]
mountain	la montagne [la montanyer]
museum	le musée [ler moozai]
nature reserve	le parc national [ler park naseeyonal]
the old town	la vieille ville [la veeyai veel]
painter	le peintre [ler pantr]
painting	la peinture [la pantoor]
palace	le palais [ler palai]
picture	le tableau [ler tablo]
queen	la reine [la ren]
religion	la religion [la rerleejeeyon]
restoration	la restauration [la restorassyon]
ruin	la ruine [la rween]
scenery, countryside	le paysage [ler paisaj]
sculptor	le sculpteur [ler skooltuhr]
sculpture	la sculpture [la skooltoor]
service *(rel)*	l'office *m* [lofeess]
sights	les curiosités *f* [lai kooreeyoseetai]
sightseeing tour of the town/city	le tour de ville [ler toor der veel]
square	la place [la plass]
tour	la visite [la veezeet]
tower	la tour [la toor]
town hall	la mairie [la mairee]
vantage point	le point de vue [ler pwand voo]
waterfall	la chute (d'eau) [la shoot (doe)]
woods, forest	la forêt [la forai]
zoo	le zoo [ler zo]

What's on the menu?

EATING OUT

Could you show me ...?	Vous pourriez m'indiquer... [voo pooreeyai mandeekai]
a good restaurant	un bon restaurant? [an bon raisteron]
a restaurant with local specialities	un bon restaurant du coin? [an bon raisteron du kwan]
I'd like to reserve a table for four for this evening, please?	Je voudrais retenir une table pour ce soir, pour quatre personnes. [jvoodrai rertneer oon tabl poor ser swar poor kat pairson]
Is this table/seat free?	Est-ce que cette table/place est libre? [es ker set tabl/plass ai leebr]
I'd like a table for two/three people.	Je voudrais une table pour deux/trois personnes. [jvoodrai oon tabl poor der/trwa pairson]
Where are the toilets, please?	Où sont les W.-C., s.v.p.? [oo son lai vaisai seel voo plai]
Cheers!	A votre santé [a votr sontai]/ A la vôtre. [a la votr]
Do you mind if I smoke?	Je peux fumer? [jper foomai]

ORDERING — COMMANDE [komond]

Could I have the menu, please.	S'il vous plaît Monsieur/Madame/Mademoiselle, la carte. [seel voo plai mer syer/madam/madmwazell la kart]
What can you recommend?	Qu'est-ce que vous me conseillez? [kes ker voom konsayai]
What would you like as a starter/for your main course/for dessert?	Qu'est-ce que vous prendrez comme hors-d'œuvre/plat principal/dessert? [kes ker voo prondrai kom orduhvr/pla pranseepal/daisair]
I'll have ...	Je prendrai ... [jer prondrai]
I'm afraid we've run out of ...	Nous n'avons malheureusement plus de ... [noo navon maluhrerzmon ploo der]

29

What would you like to drink?	Qu'est-ce que vous désirez comme boisson(s)? [kes_ker voo daizeerai kom bwason]
A glass of ..., please.	Un verre de ..., s.v.p. [an vair der ... seel voo plai]
A bottle of/Half a bottle of ..., please.	Une bouteille/Une demi-bouteille de ..., s.v.p. [oon bootai/oon dermeebootai der ... seel voo plai]

COMPLAINTS — RECLAMATIONS [raiklamaseeyon]

Have you forgotten my ...?	Vous pensez à mon/ma/mes ..., n'est-ce pas? [voo ponsai a mon/ma/mai ... ness_pa]
I didn't order that.	Ce n'est pas ce que j'ai commandé. [snai pa sker jai komondai]
Fetch the manager, please.	Allez chercher le patron, je vous prie. [alai shairshail patron jer voo pree]

COULD I HAVE THE BILL, PLEASE? — L'ADDITION, S.V.P. [ladeeseeyon seel voo plai]

All together, please.	Je paie le tout. [jer pai ler too]
Separate bills, please.	Vous faites des notes séparées, s.v.p. [voo fet dai not saiparai seel voo plai]
That's for you.	Voilà pour vous. [vwala poor voo]
Keep the change.	C'est bon, vous gardez tout. [sai bon voo gardai too]

How would you like your meat?

well done	bien cuit [beeyan kwee]
medium	à point [a pwan]
rare	saignant [sainyon]

The French tend to eat their meat quite rare. If you want your meat to be more thoroughly cooked, make sure you ask for it to be well done (*«bien cuit»*).

to bake	cuire au four [kweer o foor]
to boil	bouillir [booyeer]
breakfast	le petit déjeuner [ler ptee daijuhnai] → p. 33
children's portion	la portion pour enfants [la porseeyon poor_onfon]
cold	froid [frwa]
cook	le cuisinier/la cuisinière [ler kweezeeneeyai/la kweezeeneeyair]
to cook	faire cuire [fair kweer]
cup	la tasse [la tass]
cutlery	les couverts *m* [lai koovair]
dessert	le dessert [ler daisair] → p. 38
diabetic	le diabétique [ler deeyabeteek]
dinner	le dîner [ler deenai]
dish (of the day)	le plat (du jour) [ler pla (doo joor)]
drink	la boisson [la bwasson] → p. 39
fishbone	l'arête *f* [larett]
fork	la fourchette [la foorshet]
fresh	frais/fraîche [frai/fresh]
fried	frit/e [free/freet]
garlic	l'ail *m* [laeey]
glass	le verre [ler vair]
gravy	le jus (de la viande) [ler ju (der la viond)]
home-made	(fait/e) maison [(fai/fet) maizon]
starter	le hors-d'œuvre [ler orduhvr], l'entrée [lontrai]
hot (temp.)	très chaud [trai sho]
hot (spicy)	fort, e [for, fort]
knife	le couteau [ler kooto]
lemon	le citron [la seetron]
lunch	le déjeuner [ler daijuhnai]
main course	le plat principal [ler pla praiseepal] → p. 36
menu	la carte [la kart] → p. 33
mustard	la moutarde [la mootard]
napkin	la serviette [la sairveeyet]
oil	l'huile *f* [lweel]
order	la commande [la komond]
pepper	le poivre [ler pwavr]
plate	l'assiette *f* [lasseeyet]
portion	la portion [la porseeyon]
raw	cru/e [kroo]
roast	rôti/e [rotee]
salt	le sel [ler sel]
sauce	la sauce [la soss]
to season	assaisonner [asaizonai]
set meal/menu	le menu [ler mernoo]
spice	l'épice *f* [laipeess]

side-dishes	les accompagnements [laiz_akompanyermon]
smoked	fumé/e [foomai]
soup	la soupe [la soop] → p. 33
sour	aigre [aigr]
speciality	la spécialité [la spaiseeyaleetai]
spoon	la cuillère [la kweeyair]
straw	la paille [la paeey]
sugar	le sucre [ler sookr]
sweet	doux/douce [doo/doos]
sweetener	les sucrettes *f* [lai sookrett]
tip	le pourboire [ler poorbwar]
toothpick	le cure-dents [ler koordon]
tough	dur/e [door]
vegetarian	végétarien/végétarienne [vaijaitareeyan/vaijaitareeyen]
vinegar	le vinaigre [ler veenaigr]
waitress	la serveuse [la sairverz]
water	l'eau *f* [lo]
well-done	bien cuit [beeyan kwee]

Wine drinking

France is not just one of the largest wine producing countries, but also one of the greatest consumers. Bear in mind, however, that the French only drink wine with their meals. There isn't a "wine bar" culture as such, and you won't normally see any of the locals ordering a glass of wine at a bar or café without some food to accompany it.
If you are invited over to dinner by a French person, it is more usual to take a bunch of flowers or a special *gateau* from a *patisserie* rather than a bottle of wine.

Carte
Menu

Petit déjeuner	Breakfast
café noir [kafai nwar]	black coffee
café au lait [kafai o lai]	white coffee
décaféiné [daikafeenai]	decaffeinated coffee
thé au lait/au citron [tai o lai/o seetron]	tea with milk/lemon
tisane [teezan]	herbal tea
chocolat [shokola]	drinking chocolate
jus de fruit [jood frwee]	fruit juice
œuf mollet [uhf molai]	soft-boiled egg
œufs brouillés [er brooeeyai]	scrambled egg
œufs au plat avec du lard [erf o pla avek doo lar]	fried eggs with bacon
pain/petits pains/toasts [pan/ptee pan/tost]	bread/rolls/toast
croissant [krwason]	croissant
beurre [buhr]	butter
fromage [fromaj]	cheese
charcuterie [sharkootree]	cold meats such as ham, salami, pâté etc.
jambon [jonbon]	ham
miel [meeyel]	honey
confiture [konfeetoor]	jam
musli [mooslee]	muesli
céréales au lait [sairayal o lai]	cereals with milk
yaourt [yaoort]	yogurt
fruits [frwee]	Fruit → p.38

Potages et soupes	Soups
bisque d'écrevisses [beesk daikrervees]	lobster bisque
bouillabaisse [booeeyabais]	spicy fish soup from southern France
consommé de poulet [konsomaid poolai]	chicken consommé (broth)
potage au cresson [potaj o kraison]	cress soup
soupe à l'oignon [soop a lonyon]	French onion soup
soupe de poisson [soop der pwason]	fish soup
soupe à la tortue [soop a la tortoo]	turtle soup
velouté d'asperges [verlootai daspairj]	cream of asparagus soup

Hors-d'œuvre	Hors-d'œuvres
asperges à la crème [aspairj a la krem]	asparagus with cream sauce
avocat vinaigrette [avoka veenaigret]	avocado vinaigrette
cœurs d'artichauts [kuhr darteesho]	artichoke hearts
crudités variées [kroodeetai vareeyai]	raw vegetable/mixed salad
filets de harengs [feelai der aron]	herring fillets
jambon cru [jonbon kroo]	cured ham
jambon fumé [jonbon foomai]	smoked ham
melon au porto [merlon o porto]	melon with port
pâté de campagne [patai der konpanyer]	farmhouse pâté
pâté de foie [pataid fwa]	liver pâté
rillettes [reeyet]	rillettes (a coarse pâté made from pork, goose, duck or rabbit)
salade niçoise [salad neeswaz]	salad niçoise (lettuce, tomatoes, egg, cheese, olives, tuna, anchovies)
sardines à l'huile [sardeen a lweel]	sardines in oil
saumon fumé [somon foomai]	smoked salmon
terrine de canard [taireen der kanar]	duck pâté

Entrées	Starters
bouchées à la reine [booshai a la ren]	chicken vol-au-vent
croque Monsieur [krok mer_syer]	croque Monsieur (toast with ham and melted cheese)
croque Madame [krok madam]	like "croque Monsieur" but with an egg
cuisses de grenouilles [kwees der grernooeey]	frogs legs
escargots à la bourguignonne [eskargo a la boorgeenyon]	snails in garlic butter
omelette aux champignons [omlet o shonpeenyon]	mushroom omelette
pied de porc [peeyaid por]	pig's trotters
quiche lorraine [keesh lorain]	quiche lorraine
tête de veau vinaigrette [tet der vo veenaigret]	calf's head in vinaigrette sauce
tripes [treep]	tripe

Viandes	Meat
agneau [anyo]	lamb
bœuf [buhf]	beef
mouton [mooton]	mutton

porc [por]	pork
veau [vo]	veal
bifteck [beefteck]	steak
blanquette de veau [blonkett der vo]	veal stew
bœuf bourguignon [buhf boorgeenyon]	boeuf bourguignon (beef in red-wine sauce)
cassoulet [kasoolai]	cassoulet (casserole of butter beans, poultry and other meat)
cochon de lait [koshond lai]	suckling pig
cœur [kuhr]	heart
côte de bœuf [kot der buhf]	rib of beef
entrecôte [ontrerkot]	(entrecôte steak) ribsteak
épaule [aipol]	shoulder
escalope de veau [aiskalop der vo]	veal escalope
filet de bœuf [feelaid buhf]	fillet steak
foie [fwa]	liver
gigot d'agneau [jeego danyo]	leg of lamb
grillades [greeyad]	mixed grill
jarret de veau [jaraid vo]	veal knuckle
langue [long]	tongue
pieds de cochon [peeyaid koshon]	pig's trotters
paupiettes [popeeyet]	meat parcels (thin slices of meat rolled, stuffed and tied)
rognons [ronyon]	kidneys
rôti [rotee]	roast
sauté de veau [sotaid vo]	sauté of veal
steak au poivre [staik_o pwavr]	pepper steak
steak tartare [staik tartar]	raw minced steak seasoned and garnished

Volailles et gibier / Poultry and game

canard à l'orange [kanar a loronj]	duck à l'orange
civet de lièvre [seevai der leeyevr]	jugged hare
coq au vin [koko van]	coq au vin (chicken in red wine sauce)
dinde aux marrons [dand o maron]	turkey with chestnuts
faisan [ferzon]	pheasant
lapin chasseur [lapan shasuhr]	rabbit in tomato, mushroom and onion sauce
oie aux marrons [wa o maron]	goose with chestnut stuffing
perdrix [pairdree]	partridge
pigeons [peejon]	pidgeon
pintade [pantad]	guinea-fowl
poule au riz [pool o ree]	chicken with rice
poulet rôti [poolai rotee]	roast chicken
sanglier [songlyai]	wild boar

Crustacés et coquillages — Shellfish

Crustacés et coquillages	Shellfish
coquilles Saint-Jacques [kokeey sanjak]	scallops
crevettes [krervet]	prawns, shrimps
écrevisse [aikrervees]	crayfish
homard [omar]	lobster
huîtres [weetr]	oysters
langouste au gratin [longoost_o gratan]	crayfish au gratin (cheese-topping)
langoustines [longoosteen]	scampi
moules [mool]	mussels
plateau de fruits de mer [plato der frwee der mair]	seafood platter

Poissons	Fish

Poissons de mer — **Salt-water fish**

aiglefin [aiglerfan]	haddock
cabillaud [kabeeyo]	cod
calmar frit [kalmar free]	fried squid
colin [kolan]	hake
daurade [dorad]	sea bream
hareng [aron]	herring
lotte (de mer) [lot (der mair)]	monkfish
loup de mer [loo der mair]	bass
maquereau [makro]	mackerel
morue [moroo]	cod
rouget [roojai]	mullet
sole au gratin [sol o gratan]	sole au gratin
turbot [toorbo]	turbot

Poissons d'eau douce — **Fresh-water fish**

anguille [ongeey]	eel
brochet au bleu [broshai o bler]	blue pike
carpe [karp]	carp
perche [pairsh]	perch
petite friture [pteet freetoor]	small deep-fried fish
quenelles de brochet [kernell der broshai]	pike quenelles (poached pike)
sandre [sondr]	pike/perch
truite meunière [trweet merneeyair]	trout meunière (coated in flour, then fried in butter)

Butter in your spinach?

You might need to do this after your holiday...but don't worry if you hate spinach: *«mettre du beurre dans les épinards»* [metr doo buhr don laiz aipeenar] simply means *"to put money in the bank"*.

Légumes	Vegetables
choucroute [shookroot]	sauerkraut (pickled cabbage)
chou-fleur [shoofluhr]	cauliflower
endives au gratin [ondeev o gratan]	chicory au gratin
épinards [aipeenar]	spinach
fenouil [fernooeey]	fennel
macédoine de légumes [masaidwan der laigoom]	mixed, diced vegetables
petits pois [ptee pwa]	peas
pommes de terre sautées [pom der tair sotai]	sautéed potatoes
pommes dauphine/pommes duchesse [pom dofeen/pom dooshess]	potato croquettes
pommes natures [pom natoor]	boiled potatoes
ratatouille niçoise [ratatooeey neeswaz]	ratatouille (mixed vegetables such as tomatoes, red/green peppers, aubergine etc.)
tomates farcies [tomat farsee]	stuffed tomatoes

Pâtes et riz	Pasta and rice
macaronis [makaronee]	macaroni
nouilles [nooeey]	noodles
riz au curry [ree o kooree]	curried rice

Fromages	Cheese
fromage blanc [fromaj blon]	fromage blanc (somewhere between cottage cheese & thick cream)
fromage de chèvre [fromaj der shevr]	goat's cheese
gruyère [grooeeyair]	Gruyère (Swiss cheese)
petit suisse [ptee swees]	small creamy cheese like thick yoghurt
roquefort [rokfor]	Roquefort (strong, blue, creamy cheese)
yaourt [yaoort]	yogurt

Desserts

baba au rhum [baba o rom]	rum baba (sponge cake)
beignets aux pommes [bainyai o pom]	apple fritter
charlotte [sharlot]	charlotte (wafer biscuits with fruit and cream)
crème Sabayon [krem sabayon]	zabaglione (sweet frothy custard)
flan [flon]	baked custard pudding with caramel
gâteau [gato]	cake
ile flottante [eel flotont]	ile flottante (stiffly beaten egg white with thin custard)
mousse au chocolat [moos o shokola]	chocolate mousse
omelette norvégienne [omlet norvaijeeyain]	baked Alaska
pain perdu [pan pairdoo]	French toast
pâtisserie maison [pateesree maizon]	home-made pastries
profiteroles [profeetrol]	profiteroles
tarte aux pommes [tart o pom]	apple tart
tarte tatin [tart tatan]	apple upside-down tart

Fruits — Fruit

abricots [abreeko]	apricots
cerises [serreez]	cherries
fraises [frez]	strawberries
framboises [fronbwaz]	raspberries
macédoine de fruits [masaidwan der frwee]	fruit salad
pêches [pesh]	peaches
poires [pwar]	pears
pommes [pom]	apples
prunes [proon]	plums
raisin [raizan]	grapes

Glaces — Ice cream

au café [o kafai]	coffee ice cream
au chocolat [o shokola]	chocolate ice cream
à la fraise [a la frez]	strawberry ice cream
à la pistache [a la peestash]	pistachio ice cream
à la vanille [a la vaneey]	vanilla ice cream
café liégeois [kafai leeyaijwa]	coffee ice cream with fresh cream
coupe maison [koop maizon]	mixed ice cream
sorbet au citron [sorbai o seetron]	lemon sorbet

Liste des Consommations
Beverages

Vin rouge et vin blanc	Red and white wines
un (verre de vin) rouge [an (vair der van) rooj]	a glass of red wine
1 quart de vin blanc [an kar der van blon]	a carafe of white wine
1 pichet de rosé [an peeshaid rozai]	20 to 50 cl of rosé
Appellation contrôlée [apelasyon kontrolai]	appellation contrôlé (label guaranteeing quality of wine)
Beaujolais [bojolai]	light, fruity red wine
Bordeaux [bordo]	classic reds and good sweet whites
Bourgogne [boorgonyer]	full-bodied wines from Burgundy
Champagne [shonpanyer]	champagne
Côtes-de-Provence [kot der provons]	a robust red wine, from Provence (also rosé)
Côtes-du-Rhône [kot doo ron]	a full-bodied red wine from the Rhone valley
vin doux [van doo]	sweet white wine
vin pétillant [van petiyon]	sparkling wine

Bière	Beer
- pression [preseeyon]	draught beer
un demi [an dmee]	25 cl, 1/2 pint
un sérieux [an saireeyer]	50 cl, pint
- bouteille [bootay]	bottled beer

«Une carafe d'eau, s.v.p.» [oon karaf do seel voo plai]

In France you can order a free carafe of tap water at any time during your meal. You'll probably find that there is one on your table anyway, as water is as much a part of a French meal as bread.

Apéritifs

	Aperitifs
Pernod [pairno] Ricard [reekar]	aniseed flavoured aperitif, called "pastis".
Suze [sooz]	gentian liqueur

Alcools et liqueurs

	Brandies and Liqueurs
Armagnac [armanyak]	brandy
Calvados [kalvados]	apple brandy
Chartreuse [shartrerz]	herbal liqueur
Framboise [fronbwaz]	raspberry liqueur
Marc [mar]	marc brandy (made from pressed grapes)
Mirabelle [meerabel]	cherry brandy
Cognac [konyak]	cognac
Cidre [seedr]	cider

Boissons sans alcool

	Alcohol-free Drinks
la bière sans alcool [la beeyair sonz_alkol]	alcohol-free beer
le petit-lait [ler pteelai]	buttermilk, whey
Jus de fruits [jood frwee]	fruit juices
la limonade [la leemonad]	lemonade
le lait [ler lai]	milk
l'eau f minérale [lo meenairal]	mineral water
le jus d'orange [ler joo doronj]	orange juice

Café et thé

	Coffee and tea
café crème [kafai krem]	coffee with cream or hot milk
café express [kafai ekspress]	espresso
café au lait [kafai o lai]	white coffee
thé nature/au lait/au citron [tai natoor/o lai seetron]	black tea/with milk/ with lemon

---

If you want an English cup of tea you need to ask for *«thé au lait»* [tai o lai]. If you ask for *«le thé»* [ler tai] you will be served black tea. Herbal tea, which is drunk as an aid to sleep, is called *«une infusion»* [oon anfoozeeyon] and a fruit tea is known as *«une tisane»* [oon teezan].

Do you accept credit cards?

open... ouvert [oovair]	closed.........	fermé [fairmai]	
closed for holidays ..... vacances jusqu'au ... [vakons joosko]			

Where can I find ...?	Où est-ce qu'on peut acheter ...? [oo es kon pert_ashtai]
Can you recommend a ... shop?	Vous pourriez m'indiquer un magasin de ...? [voo pooreeyai mandeekai an magazan der]
I'd like ...	J'aimerais ... [jaimrai]
Have you got ...?	Vous avez ...? [vooz_avai]
I'll take it.	Je le/la/les prends. [jer ler/la/lai pron]
How much is it?	Combien ça coûte? [konbeeyan sa koot]
Do you take ... eurocheques? credit cards?	Vous prenez ... [voo prernai] les eurochèques? [laiz_erroshek] les cartes de crédit? [lai kart der kraidee]

antique shop	la boutique d'antiquaire [la booteek donteekair]
baker's	la boulangerie [la boolonjree]
barber's	le salon de coiffure [ler salond kwafoor] → p.48
bookshop	la librairie [la leebrairee]
butcher's	la boucherie [la booshree]
cake shop	la pâtisserie [la pateesree]
chemist's *(for prescriptions)*	la pharmacie [la farmasee] → p.42

Old and new francs

Don't panic if you hear someone, usually an older person, quoting what seems like a horrendous price to you. In 1960, the franc was devalued and 100 old francs became 1 new franc from then on. So that's why, if you meet someone who still counts in old francs, a thousand francs becomes one hundred thousand (old) francs!

chemist's *(for toiletries)*	la droguerie [la drogree]
department store	le grand magasin [ler gron magazan]
electrician	l'électricien *m* [lailektreeseeyan] → p. 45
flea market	le marché aux puces [ler marshai o poos]
florist's	le magasin de fleuriste [ler magazan der fluhreest]
food store	l'épicerie *f* [laipeesree]
greengrocer's	le marchand de primeurs [ler marshond preemuhr]
hairdresser's	le salon de coiffure [ler salond kwafoor]
household goods	les articles ménagers [laiz_arteekl mainajai] → p. 49
jeweller's	la bijouterie [la beejootree] → p. 49
market	le marché [ler marshai]
newsagent's	le marchand de journaux [ler marshond joorno]
off-licence	le commerce de vins et spiritueux [ler komairs der van ai speereetooer]
optician's	l'opticien *m* [lopteeseeyan] → p. 50
perfumery	la parfumerie [la parfoomree]
photographic materials	le photographe [ler fotograf]
second-hand bookshop	la boutique de livres d'occasion [la booteek der leevr dokazeeyon]
shoe shop	le magasin de chaussures [ler magazand shosoor]
souvenir shop	la boutique de souvenirs [la booteek der soovneer]
supermarket	le supermarché [ler soopairmarshai]
tobacconist's	le bureau de tabac [ler byoorod taba] → p. 52
toy shop	le magasin de jouets [ler magazand jooai]
travel agency	l'agence *f* de voyages [lajons der vwaeeyaj]
wine merchant's	le marchand de vins [ler marshond van]

CHEMIST'S (FOR PRESCRIPTIONS)	LA PHARMACIE [la farmasee]
Where's the nearest chemist's (with all-night service)?	Vous pourriez m'indiquer une pharmacie (de garde), s.v.p.? [voo pooreeyai mandeekai oon farmasee (der gard) seel voo plai]
Can you give me something for ...?	Donnez-moi quelque chose contre ..., s.v.p. [donai mwa kelker shoze kontr ... seel voo plai]

You need a prescription for this.	Ce médicament n'est délivré que sur ordonnance. [ser maideekamon nai daileevrai ker soor_ordonons]

to be taken internally . . .	ingestible [anjaisteebl]
for external use only	pour l'usage externe [poor loosaj ekstairn]
before meals	avant les repas [avon lai rpa]
after meals	après les repas [aprai lai rpa]
let it melt in your mouth	laisser fondre dans la bouche [laisai fondrer don la boosh]

antibiotics	l'antibiotique *m* [lonteebeeyoteek]
aspirin	l'aspirine *f* [laspeereen]
cardiac stimulant	le médicament pour la circulation [ler maideekamon poor la seerkoolaseeyon]
condom	le préservatif [ler praizairvateef]
contraceptive pill	la pillule (anticonceptionnelle) [la peelool (onteekonsepseeyonel)]
cough mixture	le sirop contre la toux [ler seero kontr la too]
disinfectant	l'antiseptique *m* [lonteesepteek]
drops	les gouttes *f* [lai goot]
eardrops	les gouttes *f* pour les oreilles [lai goot poor laiz_oray]
eye drops	le collyre liquide [ler koleer leekeed]
gauze bandage	la gaze [la gaz]
headache tablets	les cachets *m* contre les maux de tête [lai kashai kontr lai mod tet]
insect repellent	l'insecticide *m* [lansekteeseed]
insulin	l'insuline *f* [lansooleen]
laxative	le laxatif [ler laksateef]
medicine	le médicament [ler maideekamon]
ointment for burns	la pommade contre les brûlures [la pomad kontr lai brooloor]
ointment	la pommade [la pomad]
pain-killing tablets	les cachets *m* contre la douleur [lai kashai kontr la dooluhr]
plaster	le sparadrap [ler sparadra]
prescription	l'ordonnance *f* [lordonons]
remedy	le remède [ler rermed]
sedative, tranquilizer	le tranquillisant [ler tronkeeleezon]
side effects	la réaction secondaire [la rayakseeyon sergondair]
sleeping pills	les somnifères *m* [lai somneefair]
sunburn	le coup de soleil [ler koo der solay]
suppository	les suppositoires *m* [lai soopozeetwar]

43

tablet, pill	le comprimé [ler konpreemai]
thermometer	le thermomètre [ler tairmometr]
throat lozenges	les pastilles *f* contre le mal de gorge [lai pasteey kontr ler mal der gorj]

CHEMIST'S (FOR TOILETRIES) — LA DROGUERIE [la drogree]

after-shave lotion	la lotion après-rasage [la loseeyon aprairazaj]
brush	la brosse [la bros]
comb	le peigne [ler painyer]
condom	le préservatif [ler praizairvateef]
cotton-wool	le coton hydrophile [ler koton eedrofeel]
cream	la crème [la krem]
deodorant	le déodorant [ler daiodoron]
dummy	la sucette [la soosett]
eye-shadow	le fard à paupières [ler far a popeeyair]
feeding bottle	le biberon [ler beebron]
flannel	le gant de toilette [ler gon der twalet]
hairbrush	la brosse à cheveux [la bros a shver]
lipstick	le rouge à lèvres [ler rooj a levr]
mascara	le mascara [ler maskara]
mirror	la glace [la glas]
nappies	les couches *f* [lai koosh]
paper handkerchiefs	les mouchoirs *m* en papier [lai mooshwar on papeeyai]
perfume, scent	le parfum [ler parfan]
plaster	le sparadrap [ler sparadra]
powder	la poudre [la poodr]
protection factor	l'indice *m* de protection [landees der protekseeyon]
razor	le rasoir [ler razwar]
razor-blade	la lame de rasoir [la lam der razwar]
sanitary towels	les serviettes *f* hygiéniques [lai sairveeyet eejeeyaineek]
setting lotion	le fixateur [ler feeksatuhr]
shampoo	le shampooing [ler shonpwan]
shaving-brush	le blaireau [ler blairo]
shaving-soap	le savon à barbe [ler savon a barb]
soap	le savon [ler savon]

«Passer un savon à quelqu'un»

[literally: *"to give someone a bar of soap"*] is not as friendly a gesture as you might think. This colloquial expression means *"to give someone a good dressing down"*, *"to tear strips off someone"*.

suntan lotion	la crème solaire [la krem solair]
tampons	les tampons *m* [lai tonpon]
toilet-paper	le papier hygiénique [ler papeeyai eejeeyaineek]
toothbrush	la brosse à dents [la bros a don]
toothpaste	le dentifrice [ler donteefrees]
tweezers	la pince à épiler [la pans a aipeelai]

ELECTRICAL GOODS — **L'ELECTROMENAGER** [lelektromenajai]

adapter	l'adaptateur *m* [ladaptatuhr]
battery	la pile [la peel]
cassette	la cassette [la kaset]
CD, compact disk	le CD, le (disque) compact [ler saidai, ler (deesk) konpakt]
hair-dryer	le sèche-cheveux [ler saish sherver]
headphones	les écouteurs *m* [laiz_aikootuhr]
personal stereo	le walkman® [ler wokman]
plug	la prise (mâle) [la preez (mal)]
record	le disque [ler deesk]
torch	la lampe de poche [la lonp der posh]
video camera	la caméra vidéo [la kamaira veedaio]
video cassette	la vidéocassette [la veedaiokaset]
video film	le film vidéo [ler feelm veedaio]
video recorder	le magnétoscope [ler manyetoskop]

FASHION — **LA MODE** [la mod]

Can you show me ...?	Est-ce que vous pouvez me montrer ...? [es_ker voo poovaim montrai]
Can I try it on?	Je peux l'essayer? [jper laisayai]
What size do you take?	Quelle taille faites-vous? [kel taeey fet voo]
It's too ... tight/big short/long. small/big.	Il est trop ... [eel ai tro ...] étroit/large [aitrwa/larj] court/long [koor/lon] petit/grand [ptee/gron]
It's a good fit.	Il me va bien. [eel mer va beeyan.]
I'll take it.	Je le prends. [jerl pron]
It's not quite what I wanted.	Ce n'est pas tout à fait ce que je voulais. [ser nai pa toot_a fai skerj voolai]
anorak	l'anorak *m* [lanorak]
bathing costume	le maillot de bain [ler maeeyod ban]
bikini	le bikini [ler beekeenee]
blouse	le chemisier [ler shmeezeeyai]
briefs	le slip [ler sleep]
cap	la casquette [la kasket]

Conversion of French sizes

women's dresses, suits, coats etc.							
British	32	34	36	38	40	42	44
American	30	32	34	36	38	40	42
French	38	40	42	44	46	48	50

men's suits, coats etc.						
British/American	36	38	40	42	44	46
French	46	48	50	52	54	56

shirts (collar size)											
British/American	13	13½	14	14½	15	15½	15¾	16	16½	17	17½
French		34	35	36	37	38	39	40	41	42	43	44

cardigan . . . . la veste de laine [la vest der len]
coat . . . . le manteau [ler monto]
colour . . . . la couleur [la kooluhr]
dress . . . . la robe [la rob]
gloves . . . . les gants *m* [lai gon]
handbag . . . . le sac à main [ler sak_a man]
hat . . . . le chapeau [ler shapo]
jacket . . . . la veste [la vest]
nightdress . . . . la chemise de nuit [la shmeez der nwee]
pants, knickers . . . . le slip [ler sleep]
pyjamas . . . . le pyjama [ler peejama]
raincoat . . . . l'imperméable *m* [lanpairmai_abl]
scarf . . . . le châle [ler shal]
shirt . . . . la chemise [la shmeez]
skirt . . . . la jupe [la joop]
socks . . . . les chaussettes *f* [lai shoset]
(sports)jacket . . . . la veste [la vest]
stockings . . . . les bas *m* [lai ba]
suit *(man's)* . . . . le costume [ler kostoom]
suit *(woman's)* . . . . le tailleur [ler taeeyuhr]
sweater . . . . le pull-over [ler poolovair]
swimming costume . . . . . . le maillot une pièce
                              [ler maeeyo oon peeyess]
tie . . . . la cravate [la kravat]
tights . . . . les collants *m* [lai kollon]
trousers . . . . le pantalon [ler pontalon]
umbrella . . . . le parapluie [ler paraplwee]
underwear . . . . les sous-vêtements *m* [lai soovetmon]
waistcoat . . . . le gilet [ler jeelai]

cotton	le coton [ler koton]
leather	le cuir [ler kweer]
linen	le lin [ler lan], la toile [la twal]
silk	la soie [la swa]
synthetic fibre	la fibre synthétique [la feebr santaiteek]
(terry) towelling	le tissu-éponge [ler teesooaiponj]
wool	la laine [la len]

| FOOD AND DRINK | **DES DENREES ALIMENTAIRES** [lai donrai aleemontair] |

You will find a more comprehensive vocabulary list in the
FOOD & DRINK chapter (see page 33)

What can I get you?	Vous désirez? [voo daizeerai]
I'd like ..., please.	Donnez-moi ..., s.v.p. [donai mwa ... seel voo plai]
a kilo of ...	un kilo de ... [an keelo der]
a piece of ...	un morceau de ... [an morso der]
a packet of ...	un paquet de ... [an pakai der]
a jar of ...	un verre de ... [an vair der]
a tin of ...	une boîte de ... [oon bwat der]
a bottle of ...	une bouteille de ... [oon bootay der]
a bag	un sac en plastique [an sak on plasteek]
Can I get you anything else?	Et avec ça? [ai avek sa]
No, thank you. That's all.	Non, merci. C'est tout. [non mairsee sai too]

alcohol-free beer	la bière sans alcool [la beeyair sonz_alkol]
baby food	les aliments *m* pour bébés [laiz_aleemon poor baibai]
beer	la bière [la beeyair]
biscuits	les biscuits *m* [lai beeskwee]
bread	le pain [ler pan]
butter	beurre [buhr]
cake	gâteau [gato] → p.38
cakes	les pâtisseries *f* [lai pateesree]
cheese	fromage [fromaj] → p.37
chicken	le poulet [ler poolai]
chocolate	chocolat [shokola]
coffee	le café [ler kafai] → p.33
cream	la crème [la krem]
eggs	les œufs *m* [laiz_er]
fish	le poisson [ler pwason] → p.36
flour	la farine [la fareen]
fresh	frais/fraîche [frai/fresh]
fruit	les fruits *m* [lai frwee] → p.38
health food	les aliments *m* naturels [laiz_aleemon natoorel]
ice-cream	la glace [la glas] → p.38

jam	confiture [konfeetoor]
lemonade	la limonade [la leemonad]
margarine	la margarine [la margareen]
meat	la viande [la veeyond] → p. 34
milk	le lait [ler lai]
mince, minced meat	la viande hâchée [la veeyond ashai]
mineral water	l'eau *f* minérale [lo meenairal]
noodles	nouilles [nooeey]
nuts	les noix *f* [lai nwa]
oil	l'huile *f* [lweel]
orange juice	le jus d'orange [ler joo doronj]
organic food	les aliments *m* complets [laiz_aleemon konplai]
pasta	les pâtes [lai pat]
rolls	les petits pains [lai ptee pan]
salad	la salade [la salad]
salt	le sel [ler sel]
sausages	les saucisses *f* [lai sosees]
soup	la soupe [la soop] → p. 33
sweets *(after dinner ~)*	les friandises *f* [lai freeyondeez] → p. 38
tea	le thé [ler tai] → p. 33
tea bags	le sachet de thé [ler sashaid tai]
toast	le toast [ler tost]
vegetables	les légumes *m* [lai laigoom] → p. 37
wine	le vin [ler van] → p. 39
yoghurt	yaourt [yaoort]

HAIRDRESSER'S	**LE SALON DE COIFFURE** [ler salond kwafoor]
Can I make an appointment for tomorrow?	Est-ce que je peux prendre rendez-vous pour demain? [es_kerj per prondr rondaivoo poor dman]
Shampoo and blow dry, please.	Shampooing et brushing, s.v.p. [shonpwan ai brersheeng seel voo plai]
Wash and cut/Dry cut, please.	Une coupe avec/sans shampooing, s.v.p. [oon koop avek/son shonpwan seel voo plai]
A bit shorter/ Not too short/ Very short, please.	Un peu plus courts [an per ploo koor]/ Pas trop courts [pa tro koor]/ Très courts [trai koor], s.v.p. [seel voo plai]
I'd like a shave, please.	Un rasage, s.v.p. [an razaj seel voo plai]
Would you trim my moustache/beard, please?	Vous me taillez la moustache/la barbe, s.v.p. [voom taeeyai la moostash/la barb seel voo plai]
Thank you. That's fine.	Merci beaucoup. Ça va très bien. [mairsee bokoo sa va trai beeyan]

beard	la barbe [la barb]
to blow dry	faire un brushing [fair an brersheeng]
to comb	peigner [painyai]
curlers	les bigoudis *m* [lai beegoodee]
curls	les boucles *f* [lai bookl]
dandruff	les pellicules *f* [lai peleekyool]
to do someone's hair	coiffer [kwafai]
to dye	faire une coloration [fair oon koloraseeyon]
fringe	la frange [la fronj]
hair	les cheveux [lai shver]
haircut	la coupe [la koop]
hairstyle	la coiffure [la kwafoor]
highlights	les mèches [lai mesh]
moustache	la moustache [la moostash]
parting	la raie [la rai]
perm	la permanente [la pairmanont]
shampoo	le shampooing [ler shonpwan]
to set	faire une mise en plis [fair oon meez on plee]
to tint	faire un rinçage [fair an ranzaj]
wig	la perruque [la pairook]

HOUSEHOLD GOODS — LES ARTICLES MENAGERS [laiz arteekl mainajai]

bottle-opener	l'ouvre-bouteilles *m* [loovrerbootay]
candles	les bougies *f* [lai boojee]
charcoal	le charbon de bois [ler sharbond bwa]
corkscrew	le tire-bouchon [ler teerbooshon]
cutlery	les couverts *m* [lai koovair]
grill	le gril [ler greel]
methylated spirits	l'alcool *m* à brûler [lalkol a broolai]
paraffin	le pétrole [ler paitrol]
pocket knife	le couteau de poche [ler kootod posh]
sunshade	le parasol [ler parasol]
tin-opener	l'ouvre-boîtes *m* [loovrerbwat]

JEWELLER'S — LA BIJOUTERIE [la beejootree]

My watch doesn't work.	Ma montre ne marche plus. [ma montr ner marsh ploo]
Could you have a look at it?	Vous pourriez la regarder, s.v.p.? [voo pooreeyai la rgardai seel voo plai]
I'd like a nice souvenir/ present.	Je voudrais un joli souvenir/cadeau. [jvoodrai an jolee soovneer/kado]

bracelet	le bracelet [ler braslai]
brooch	la broche [la brosh]
costume jewellery	les bijoux *m* fantaisie
	[lai beejoo fontaizee]
crystal	le cristal [ler kreestal]
earrings	les boucles *f* d'oreilles
	[lai bookl doray]
gold	l'or *m* [lor]
jewellery	les bijoux *m* [lai beejoo]
necklace	le collier [ler koleeyai]
pearl	la perle [la pairl]
pendant	le pendentif [ler pondonteef]
ring	la bague [la bag]
silver	l'argent *m* [larjon]
wrist watch	la montre-bracelet [la montr braslai]

OPTICIAN'S

L'OPTICIEN [lopteeseeyan]

Could you repair these glasses for me, please.
Je voudrais faire réparer ces lunettes. [jer voodrai fair raiparai sai loonett]

I'm short-sighted/long-sighted.
Je suis myope/hypermétrope. [jer swee meeyop/eepairmaitrop]

What's your sight measureent?
Quelle est votre acuité visuelle? [kel_ai votr akweetai veezooel]

... in the right eye, ... in the left eye
Œil droit ..., œil gauche ... [uh_ee drwa ... uh_ee goshe]

When can I pick up the glasses?
Quand est-ce que je peux venir chercher les lunettes? [kont_es_kerj per vneer shairshai lai loonett]

I need some cleansing solution ...
    for hard/soft contact lenses.
Il me faudrait du liquide de nettoyage [eel mer fodrai doo leekeed der naitwaeeyaj]
    pour lentilles dures/molles. [poor lonteey door/mol]

I'm looking for ...
    some sunglasses.

    some binoculars.
Je voudrais ... [jvoodrai]
    des lunettes de soleil. [dai loonett der solay]
    des jumelles. [dai joomell]

PHOTOGRAPHIC MATERIALS	**LE PHOTOGRAPHE** [ler fotograf]

I'd like ...
a film for this camera.

J'aimerais ... [jemrai]
une pellicule pour cet appareil.
[oon peleekyool poor set aparay]

a colour film (for slides).

une pellicule couleur (pour diapos).
[oon peleekyool kooluhr (poor deeyapo)]

Could you put the film in the camera for me, please?

Vous pourriez mettre la pellicule dans l'appareil, s.v.p.? [voo pooreeyai metr la peleekyool don laparay seel voo plai]

The view-finder/shutter doesn't work.

Le viseur/Le déclencheur ne fonctionne plus. [ler veezuhr/ler daiklonshuhr ner fonkseeyon ploo]

Can you mend it?

Vous pouvez réparer ça, s.v.p.?
[voo poovai raiparai sa seel voo plai]

black and white film	le film en noir et blanc [ler feelm on nwar ai blon]
colour film	la pellicule couleur [la peleekyool kooluhr]
film speed	la sensibilité [la sonseebeeleetai]
flash, flashcube	le flash [ler flash]
lens, objective	l'objectif *m* [lobjekteef]
shutter	le déclencheur [ler daiklonshuhr]

SHOE SHOP	**LE MAGASIN DE CHAUSSURES** [ler magazand shosoor]

I'd like a pair of ... shoes.

Je voudrais une paire de ...
[jvoodrai oon pair der]

What size do you take?

Quelle pointure faites-vous?
[kel pwantyoor fet voo]

They're too narrow/wide.

Elles sont trop petites/grandes.
[el son tro pteet/grond]

boots	les bottes *f* [lai bot]
children's shoes	les chaussures d'enfants [lai shosoor donfon]
rubber boots, wellingtons	les bottes *f* en caoutchouc [lai bot on kaootshoo]
sandals	les sandales *f* [lai sondal]
shoe	la chaussure [la shosoor]
shoe polish	le cirage [ler seeraj]
trainers	les tennis *f* [lai tainee]

Conversion of Shoe Sizes

Brit./American	2½	3½	4	5	6	6½	7	8	9	9½
French	35	36	37	38	39	40	41	42	43	44

STATIONER'S | LA PAPETERIE [la papaitree]

Do you sell English news-papers/magazines?	Est-ce-que vous vendez des journaux/magazines anglais? [es_ker voo vondai dai magazeen onglai]
I'd like ...	Je voudrais ... [jvoodrai]

ballpoint pen	le stylo à bille [ler steelo a beey]
envelope	l'enveloppe *f* [lonvlop]
eraser	la gomme [la gom]
guide	le guide touristique [ler geed tooreesteek]
magazine	l'illustré *m* [leeloostrai]
magazine	le magazine [ler magazeen]
map	la carte (géographique) [la kart (jaiografeek)]
map of walks	la carte de randonnée [la kart der rondonai]
newspaper	le journal [ler joornal]
notepad	le bloc-notes [ler bloknot]
paperback	le livre de poche [ler leevr der posh]
picture postcard	la carte postale illustrée [la kart postal eeloostrai]
playing cards	le jeu de cartes [ler jerd kart]
road map	la carte routière [la kart rooteeyair]
sketchbook	le bloc de papier à dessin [ler blok der papeeyai a daisan]
stamp	le timbre [ler tanbr]
town map	le plan (de la ville) [ler plon (der la veel)]

TOBACCONIST'S | LE BUREAU DE TABAC [ler byoorod taba]

A packet/carton of filter/filterless ... cigarettes, please.	Un paquet/Une cartouche de ... filtre/sans filtre, s.v.p. [an pakai/oon kartoosh der ... feeltr/son feeltr seel voo plai]
Ten cigars/cigarillos, please.	Dix cigares/cigarillos, s.v.p. [dee seegar/seegareeyo seel voo plai]
A packet/tin of cigarette/pipe tobacco, please.	Un paquet/Une boîte de tabac pour cigarettes/pipes, s.v.p. [an pakai/oon bwat der taba poor seegarett/peep seel voo plai]
A box of matches/A lighter, please.	Une boîte d'allumettes/Un briquet, s.v.p. [oon bwat daloomet/an breekai seel voo plai]

A double room, please

Excuse me, can you tell me where there is ..., please?
Pardon, Mme/Mlle/M., vous pourriez m'indiquer ...? [pardon madam/ madmwazell/mer_syer voo pooreeyai mandeekai]

  a hotel
    un hôtel [ann_otel]

  a guest-house
    une pension de famille
    [oon ponseeyond fameey]

Is there a youth hostel/a campsite here?
Est-ce qu'il y a une auberge de jeunesse/un terrain de camping ici?
[es_keel_eeya oon_obairj der juhness/an tairand konpeeng eesee]

HOTEL

RECEPTION DESK	**A LA RECEPTION** [a la raisepseeyon]

I've reserved a room. My name's ...
J'ai réservé une chambre chez vous. Je m'appelle ... [jai raisairvai oon shonbr shai voo. jer mapell]

Have you got any vacancies?
Est-ce que vous avez encore des chambres de libres? [es_ker vooz_avai onkor dai shonbr der leebr]

  ... for one night.
    ... pour une nuit. [poor oon nwee]

  ... for two days.
    ... pour deux jours. [poor der joor]

  ... for a week.
    ... pour une semaine. [poor oon smen]

No, I'm afraid we're full up.
Non, Mme/Mlle/M. Malheureusement, nous sommes «complet».
[non madam/madmwazell/mer_syer maluhrerzmon noo som konplai]

Yes, what sort of room would you like?
Oui, qu'est-ce que vous désirez comme chambre?
[wee kes_ker voo daizeerai kom shonbr]

  a single room
    une chambre pour une personne
    [oon shonbr poor oon pairson]

  a double room
    une chambre pour deux personnes
    [oon shonbr poor der pairson], une chambre double [oon shonbr doobl]

with a shower	avec douche [avek doosh]
with a bath	avec salle de bains [avek sal der ban]
a quiet room	une chambre calme [oon shonbr kalm]
with a view of the sea	avec vue sur la mer [avek voo soor la mair]

| Can I see the room? | Est-ce que je peux voir la chambre? [es_kerj per vwar la shonbr] |
| Can you put a third bed in the room? | Est-ce que vous pouvez installer un troisième lit? [es_ker voo poovai anstalai an trwazeeyem lee] |

How much is the room with ...	Quel est le prix de la chambre, ... [kel_ai ler preed la shonbr]
breakfast?	petit déjeuner compris? [ptee daijuhnai konpree]
breakfast and evening meal?	en demi-pension? [on dmee ponseeyon]
full board?	en pension complète? [on ponseeyon konplet]

| What time's breakfast? | Le petit déjeuner, c'est à partir de quelle heure? [ler ptee daijuhnai sait_a parteer der kel_uhr] |
| Where's the restaurant? | Où est la salle à manger? [oo ai la sal a monjai] |

Breakfast: see FOOD & DRINK, Menu → p.33

| Please wake me at ... o'clock in the morning. | Réveillez-moi à ... heures, demain matin, s.v.p. [raivaiyai mwa a ... uhr dman matan seel voo plai] |
| My key, please. | Ma clé, s.v.p. [ma klai seel voo plai] |

COMPLAINTS | ## RECLAMATIONS [raiklamaseeyon]

The room hasn't been cleaned.	Ma chambre n'a pas été nettoyée. [ma shonbr na paz_aitai naitwaeeyai]
The shower ...	La douche ... [la doosh]
The lavatory ...	La chasse d'eau ... [la shas doe]
The heating ...	Le chauffage ... [ler shofaj]
The light ...	L'éclairage ... [laiklairaj]
doesn't work.	ne fonctionne pas. [ner fonkseeyon pa]
There's no (warm) water.	Il n'y a pas d'eau (chaude). [eel neeya pa doe (shode)]
The toilet/wash-basin is blocked up.	Les W.-C. sont bouchés/Le lavabo est bouché. [lai vaisai son booshai/ler lavabo ai booshai]

54

DEPARTURE	LE DEPART [ler daipar]
I'm leaving this evening/ tomorrow at ... o'clock.	Je pars ce soir/demain à ... heures. [jer par ser swar/dman a ... uhr]
I'd like my bill, please.	Est-ce que vous pouvez préparer ma note, s.v.p.? [es_ker voo poovai praiparai ma not seel voo plai]
Do you accept euro-cheques?	Est-ce que vous prenez les eurochèques? [es_ker voo prernai laiz_erroshek]
Can I pay by credit card?	Vous acceptez les cartes de crédit? [vooz_akseptai lai kart der kredee]
Thank you very much for everything. Goodbye!	Merci pour tout! Au revoir! [mairsee poor too o rvwar]

adapter	la prise multiple [la preez moolteepl]
baby-sitting service	la garderie [la garderree]
bathroom	la salle de bains [la sal der ban]
bed	le lit [ler lee]
bed linen	la literie [la leetree]
bedside table	la table de nuit [la tabl der nwee]
breakfast	le petit déjeuner [ler ptee daijuhnai]
breakfast-room	la salle de petit déjeuner [la sal der ptee daijuhnai]
chambermaid	la femme de chambre [la fam der shonbr]
to clean	nettoyer [naitwaeeyai]
cot	le lit d'enfant [ler lee donfon]
cupboard	l'armoire f [larmwar]
dining room	la salle à manger [la sal a monjai]
dinner	le dîner [ler deenai]
floor, storey	l'étage m [laitaj]
full board	la pension complète [la ponseeyon konplet]
guest house	la pension de famille [la ponseeyond fameey]
half board	la demi-pension [la dmeeponseeyon]
heating	le chauffage [ler shofaj]
high season	la pleine saison [la plen saizon]
key	la clé [la klai]
lamp	la lampe [la lonp]
lavatory, toilet	les toilettes f [lai twalet]
end of the season	l'arrière-saison f [larreeyair_saizon]
beginning of the season	l'avant-saison f [lavonsaizon]
lunch	le déjeuner [ler daijuhnai]
mirror	la glace [la glas]
pillow	l'oreiller m [loraiyai]
plug	la prise (mâle) [la preez (mal)]
porter	le portier [ler porteeyai]
radio	la radio [la radeeyo]

reading lamp	la lampe de chevet [la lonp der shvai]
lobby	le hall [ler ol]
reception	la réception [la raisepseeyon]
reservation	la réservation [la raizairvaseeyon]
room	la chambre [la shonbr]
safe	le coffre-fort [ler kofrerfor]
shower	la douche [la doosh]
tap	le robinet [ler robeenai]
toilet-paper	le papier hygiénique [ler papeeyai eejeeyaineek]
towel	la serviette de toilette [la sairveeyet der twalet]
(wall)socket	la prise (femelle) [la preez (fermel)]
washbasin	le lavabo [ler lavabo]
water	l'eau f [lo]
warm water	l'eau chaude [lo shode]
cold water	l'eau froide [lo frwad]
window	la fenêtre [la fernetr]

RENTED ACCOMMODATION

Is electricity/water included in the price?	Est-ce que l'eau et l'électricité sont comprises dans le loyer? [es_ker lo ai lailektreeseetai son konpreez donl lwaeeyai]
Are pets allowed?	Est-ce que les animaux domestiques sont admis? [es_ker laiz_aneemo domaisteek sont_admee]
Where can we pick up the keys to the house?	A qui faut-il s'adresser pour avoir la clé de la maison? [a kee fot_eel sadressai poor avwar la klaid la maizon]
Do we have to clean the flat before we leave?	Est-ce que nous devons faire nous-mêmes le nettoyage de fin de séjour? [es_ker noo dvon fair noo mem ler naitwaeeyaj der fand saijoor]

additional costs, extras	les charges f [lai sharj]
bedroom	la chambre à coucher [la shonbr a kooshai]
bungalow	le bungalow [ler bangalo]
bunk bed	le lit superposé [ler lee soopairposai]
coffee machine	la machine à café [la masheen a kafai]
cooker, stove	la cuisinière [la kweezeeneeyair]
day of arrival	le jour de l'arrivée [ler joor der lareevai]
electricity	le courant (électrique) [ler kooron (ailektreek)]
flat/apartment	l'appartement m [lapartermon]

56

holiday camp	le village de vacances [ler veelaj der vakons]
holiday flat	l'apartment de vacances [lapartermon der vakons]
holiday home	la maison de vacances/de campagne [la maizond vakons/konpanyer]
kitchenette	le coin-cuisine [ler kwankweezeen]
landlord	le propriétaire (de la maison) [ler propreeyetair (der la maizon)]
to let, to rent	louer [looai]
pets	les animaux *m* domestiques [laiz_aneemo domaisteek]
refrigerator, fridge	le réfrigérateur [ler raifreejairatuhr]
rent	la location [la lokaseeyon]
rubbish	les ordures *f* [laiz_ordoor]
sofa bed	la banquette-lit [la bonketlee]
toaster	le grille-pain [ler greeypan]
washing machine	la machine à laver [la masheen_a lavai]

CAMPING

Have you got room for another caravan/tent?	Est-ce que vous avez encore de la place pour une caravane/une tente? [es_ker vooz_avai onkor der la plass poor oon karavan/oon tont]
How much does it cost per day and person?	Quel est le tarif par jour et par personne? [kel_ail tareef par joor ai par pairson]
What's the charge for ... cars? caravans? mobile homes? tents?	Quel est le tarif pour ... [kel_ail tareef poor] les voitures? [lai vwatoor] les caravanes? [lai karavan] les camping-cars? [lai konpeengkar] les tentes? [lai tont]
We'll be staying for ... days/ weeks.	Nous pensons rester ... jours/semaines. [noo ponson raistai ... joor/smen]
Is there a food-store here?	Est-ce qu'il y a une épicerie? [es_keel_eeya oon_aipeesree]
Where are the ... toilets? washrooms? showers?	Où sont ... [oo son] les W.-C.? [lai vaisai] les lavabos? [lai lavabo] les douches? [lai doosh]
Are there electric points here?	Est-ce qu'il y a des prises de courant dans le camp? [es_keel_eeya dai preez der kooron donl kon]

booking	la réservation [la raizairvaseeyon]
camper van	le camping-car [ler konpeeng kar]
camping	le camping [ler konpeeng]
campsite	le (terrain de) camping [ler (tairan der) konpeeng]
caravan	le caravane [karavan]
stove	le réchaud [ler raisho]
drinking-water	l'eau f potable [lo potabl]
electric point	la prise de courant [la preez der kooron]
electricity	le courant (électrique) [ler kooron (ailektreek)]
gas canister	la bouteille de gaz [la bootay der gaz]
gas-cooker	le réchaud à gaz [ler raisho a gaz]
(hire) charge	le tarif d'utilisation [ler tareef dooteeleezaseeyon]
rental	le tarif de location [ler tareef der lokaseeyon]
hire	louer [looai]
paraffin lamp	la lampe à pétrole [la lonp a paitrol]
plug	la prise (mâle) [la preez (mal)]
sink	le lavabo pour la vaisselle [ler lavabo poor la vaisell]
tent	la tente [la tont]
tent peg	le piquet [peekai]
water	l'eau f [lo]

YOUTH HOSTEL

Can I hire ...?	Est-ce que vous pouvez me louer ...? [es_ker voo poovaim looai]
The front door is locked at midnight.	La porte d'entrée est fermée à partir de minuit. [la port dontrai ai fairmai a parteer der meenwee]
day room	la salle commune [la sal komoon]
dormitory	le dortoir [ler dortwar]
membership card	la carte de membre [la kart der monbr]
sleeping-bag	le sac de couchage [ler sak der kooshaj]
washroom	les lavabos m [lai lavabo]
youth hostel	l'auberge f de jeunesse [lobairj der juhness]

"We haven't left the hostel yet"

«On n'est pas sorti de l'auberge!» means something like *"we're not out of the woods yet!"*

Out on the town

BAR/DISCOTHEQUE/ NIGHT-CLUB	BAR/DISCOTHEQUE/BOITE DE NUIT [bar/deeskotek/bwat der nwee]
What can we do here in the evenings?	Qu'est ce qu'on peut faire ici les soirs? [kes_kon per fair eesee lai swar]
Is there a nice pub here?	Est-ce qu'il y a un bistrot sympa, dans le coin? [es_keel_eeya an beestro sanpa donl kwan]
Where can we go dancing?	Où est ce qu'on puet aller danser? [oo es_kon per alai donsai]
Is evening dress required?	Est-ce qu'on exige une certaine tenue vestimentaire? [es_konn_aigzeej oon sairtenn ternoo vesteemontair]
One drink is included in the price of admission.	Le billet d'entrée donne droit à une consommation gratuite. [ler beeyai dontrai don drwa a oon konsomaseeyon gratweet]
A whisky and soda, please.	Un whiskey soda, s.v.p. [oon weeskee soda]
The same again.	La même chose, s.v.p. [la mem shoze seel voo plai]
This round's on me.	Je paie la tournée. [jpai la toornai]
Shall we (have another) dance?	On danse (encore une fois)? [on dons (onkor_oon fwa)]

band	l'orchestre *m* [lorkestr]
bar	le bar [ler bar]
casino	le casino [ler kazeeno]
dance music	la musique de danse [la moozeek der dons]
to dance	danser [donsai]
disc-jockey	le discjockey [ler deeskjokai]
discotheque	la discothèque [la deeskotek]
folk music	la musique traditionelle [la moozeek tradeeseeyonel]
to go out	sortir [sorteer]
live music	la musique en direct [la moozeek on deerekt]
night-club	la boîte de nuit [la bwat der nwee]
pub	le pub [ler poob]
show	le show [ler sho]

Have you got a listing of events for this week?	Vous avez le programme des spectacles de cette semaine? [vooz_avai ler program dai spektakl der set smen]
What's on at the theatre tonight?	Quelle pièce est-ce qu'on joue ce soir, au théâtre? [kel peeyess es_kon joo ser swar o taiatr]
Can you recommend a good play?	Vous pouvez m'indiquer une bonne pièce de théâtre? [voo poovai mandeekai oon bon peeyess der taiatr]
When does the performance start?	A quelle heure commence la représentation? [a kel_uhr komons la rerpraizontaseeyon]
Where can I get tickets?	Où est-ce qu'on peut prendre les billets? [oo es_kon per prondr lai beeyai]
Two tickets for this evening, please.	Deux billets pour ce soir, s.v.p. [der beeyai poor ser swar seel voo plai]
Two seats at ..., please.	Deux places à ..., s.v.p. [der plass a ... seel voo plai]
Can I have a programme, please?	Le programme, s.v.p. [ler program seel voo plai]
Where's the cloakroom?	Où est le vestiaire, s.v.p.? [oo ai ler vesteeyair seel voo plai]

advance booking	la location [la lokaseeyon]
ballet	le ballet [ler balai]
box office	la caisse [la kes]
calendar of events	le programme des spectacles [ler program dai spektakl]
cinema	le cinéma [ler seenaima]
circus	le cirque [ler seerk]
concert	le concert [ler konsair]
conductor	le chef d'orchestre [ler shef dorkestr]
festival	le festival [ler faisteeval]
film	le film [ler feelm]
opera	l'opéra *m* [lopaira]
performance	*(Kino)* la séance [la sayonss]
play	la pièce [la peeyess]
premiere	la première [la prermeeyair]
programme	le programme [ler program]
show	le spectacle [ler spektakl]
theatre	le théâtre [ler taiatr]
ticket	le billet [ler beeyai]

On the beach

AT THE SWIMMING POOL/ ON THE BEACH	A LA PISCINE / A LA PLAGE [a la peeseen/a la plaj]
Is there ... here?	Est-ce qu'il y a ... ici? [es_keel_eeya ... eesee]
an open-air pool	une piscine en plein air [oon peeseen on plan_air]
an indoor pool	une piscine couverte [oon peeseen koovairt]

Swimmers only!	Pour les nageurs seulement! [poor lai najuhr suhlmon]
No diving!	Plongeons interdits! [plonjon antairdee]
No swimming!	Baignade interdite! [bainyad antairdeet]

Are there sea-urchins/ jellyfish here?	Est-ce qu'il y a des oursins/des méduses? [es_keel_eeya daiz_oorsan/dai maidooz]
Is there a strong current?	Est-ce qu'il y a un courant violent? [es_keel_eeya an kooron veeyolon]
Is it dangerous for children?	C'est dangereux pour les enfants? [sai donjrer poor laiz_onfon]
When's low tide/high tide?	La marée basse/haute, c'est quand? [la marai bas/ot sai kon]
I'd like to rent ...	Je voudrais louer ... [jer voodrai looai]
a boat.	une barque. [oon bark]
a pair of water-skis.	des skis nautiques. [dai skee noteek]
How much is it per hour/ day?	Quel est le tarif à l'heure/à la journée? [kel_ail tareef a luhr/a la joornai]

SPORT	LE SPORT [ler spor]
What sports facilities are there here?	Qu'est-ce qu'on peut pratiquer comme sports, ici? [kes_kon per prakteekai kom spor eesee]
Is there ... here?	Est-ce qu'il y a ici ... [es_keel_eeya eesee]
a golf course	un terrain de golf? [an tairand golf]
a tennis court	un tennis? [an tainees]
Where can I go fishing?	Où est-ce qu'on peut pêcher? [oo es_kon per peshai]

61

I'd like to hire a bike ...	Je voudrais louer un vélo ... [jvoodrai looai an vailo]
for two days.	pour deux jours. [poor der joor]
for a week.	pour une semaine. [poor oon smen]
I'd like to go for a hike in the mountains.	Je voudrais faire une randonnée en montagne. [jvoodrai fair_oon rondonai on montanyer]
Can you show me an interesting route on the map?	Vous pouvez m'indiquer un itinéraire intéressant sur la carte? [voo poovai mandeekai ann_eeteenairair antairesson soor la kart]
Where can I hire ...?	Où est-ce que je peux louer ...? [oo es kerj per looai]
I'd like to attend a ... course.	Je voudrais prendre des cours de ... [jvoodrai prondr dai koor der]
Can I play too?	Je peux jouer? [jper jooai]

airbed (US), lilo(UK)	le matelas pneumatique [ler matla pnermateek]
armbands, floats	les flotteurs *m* [lai flotuhr]
athletics	l'athlétisme *m* [latlaiteesm]
ball	le ballon [ler balon]
basketball	le basket [ler baskett]
beginner	le débutant [ler daibooton]
boat hire	la location de bateaux [la lokaseeyond bato]
cable railway, funicular ..	le téléphérique [ler tailaifaireek]
canoe	le canoë [ler kanoai]
chair lift	le télésiège [ler tailaiseeyaij]
championships	le championnat [ler shonpeeyona]
contest, match	la compétition [la konpaiteeseeyon]
course	les cours *m* [lai koor]
crazy golf	le minigolf [ler meeneegolf]
crew	l'équipe *f* [laikeep]
cross-country skiing	le ski de fond [lai skee der fon]
to cycle	faire du vélo [fair doo vailo]
cycle racing	la course cycliste [la koors seekleest]
cycle tour	la randonnée cycliste [la rondonai seekleest]
defeat	la défaite [la daifett]
to dive	faire de la plongée [fair der la plonjai]
diving equipment	l'équipement *m* de plongée [laikeepmond plonjai]
diving-board	le tremplin [ler tronplan]
doubles *(tennis)*	le double [ler doobl]
draglift	le téléski [ler tailaiskee]

to draw	dessiner [daiseenai]
fishing	la pêche [la pesh]
fishing licence	le permis (de pêche) [ler pairmeed pesh]
fishing rod	la canne à pêche [la kana pesh]
football	le football [ler footbol]
football ground	le terrain de football [ler tairand footbol]
football match/game	le match de football [ler matsh der footbol]
football team	l'équipe de football [laikeep der footbol]
footpath	le chemin de randonnée [ler shmand rondonai]
to go gliding	faire du planeur [fair doo planuhr]
to go jogging, to jog	faire du jogging [fair doo djogeeng]
to go sailing	faire de la voile [fair der la vwal]
goal	le but [ler boot]
goalkeeper	le gardien de buts [ler gardeeyan der boot]
golf	le golf [ler golf]
golf club	la crosse de golf [la kros der golf]
gymnastics	la gymnastique [la jeemnasteek]
handball	le hand-ball [ler andbal]
hiking	la randonnée pédestre [la rondonai paidestr]
hockey	le hockey [okai]
ice-hockey	le hockey sur glace [ler okai soor glas]
ice-skates	les patins *m* à glace [lai patan a glas]
lifeguard	le/la surveillant(e) de baignade [soorvayon der bainyad]
to lose	perdre [pairdr]
match, game	le match [ler matsh]
motorboat	le canot automobile [ler kano otomobeel]
mountaineering	l'alpinisme *m* [lalpeeneesm]
net	le filet [ler feelai]
non-swimmer	le non-nageur [ler nonnajuhr]
nudist beach	la plage de nudistes [la plaj der noodeest]
open-air pool	une piscine en plein air [oon peeseen on plan_air]
parachuting	le parachutisme [ler parashooteesm]
pedal boat	le pédalo [ler paidalo]
programme	le programme [ler program]
race	la course [la koors]
referee	l'arbitre *m* [larbeetr]
regatta	les régates *f* [lai raigat]
result	le résultat [ler raizoolta]
to ride, to go riding	faire du cheval *f* [fair doo shval]

riding	l'équitation *f* [laikeetaseeyon]
rock-climbing	la grimp [la gramp]
rowing	(faire de) l'aviron *m* [(fair der) laveeron]
rowing-boat	la barque (à rames) [la bark (a ram)]
rubber dinghy	le canot pneumatique [ler kano pnermateek]
sailing boat	le voilier [ler vwaleeyai]
sand	le sable [ler sabl]
sauna	le sauna [ler sona]
shower	la douche [la doosh]
shuttlecock	le volant [ler volon]
singles *(tennis)*	le simple [ler sanpl]
ski	le ski [ler skee]
skiing	skier [skeeyai], faire du ski [fair doo skee]
sledge, toboggan	le traîneau [ler traino]
snorkel	le tuba [ler tooba]
soccer	*see "football"*
solarium	le solarium [ler solareeyom]
sports ground	le terrain de sport [ler tairan der spor]
sportsman/-woman	le sportif/la sportive [ler sporteef/ la sporteev]
squash	le squash [ler skwash]
start	le départ [ler daipar]
sunshade	le parasol [ler parasol]
surfboard	la planche à voile [la plonsh a vwal]
surfing	le surf [ler surf]
swimmer	le nageur / la nageuse [ler najuhr/la najerz]
swimming	nager [najai]
swimming pool	la piscine [la peeseen]
swimming pool attendant	le maître-nageur [ler maitr_najuhr]
table tennis	le tennis de table [ler tainees der tabl], le ping-pong [ler peengpong]
table-tennis bat	la batte de ping pong [bat der peengpong]
tennis	le tennis [ler tainees]
tennis racket	la raquette de tennis [la rakett der tainees]
ticket	le billet [ler beeyai]
ticket office	la caisse [la kes]
umpire	l'arbitre *m* [larbeetr]
volleyball	le volley-ball [ler volaibol]
water polo	le water-polo [ler vwatairpolo]
to win	gagner [ganyai]
win, victory	la victoire [la veektwar]
windbreak	le pare-vent [ler parvon]
(to go) windsurfing	(faire de) la planche à voile [(fair der) la plonsh a vwal]

Looking after the kids

Are there also children's portions?

Vous faites des demi-portions pour les enfants? [voo fet dai dmeeporseeyon poor laiz_onfon]

Could you please warm up the bottle?

Pourriez-vous faire chauffer le bibe-ron, s'il vous plaît? [pooreeyai voo fair shofai ler beebron seel voo plai]

Do you have a mothers' and babies' room?

Est-ce qu'il y a une nursery? [es_keeleeya oon nuhrserree]

Where can I breast feed?

Ou est-ce que je peut allaiter [oo es_kerj per alaitai]

Please bring a high chair.

Pourriez-vous apporter une chaise d'enfant, s'il vous plaît. [pooreeyai voo aportai oon shez donfon seel voo plai]

armbands	les flotteurs *m* [lai flotuhr]
baby food	aliments infantiles [aleemon anfonteel]
baby's changing table	la table à langer [la tabl a lonjai]
baby-sitter	le/la baby-sitter [ler/la baibeeseetuhr]
baby-sitting service	la garderie [la garderree]
bottle warmer	le chauffe-biberon [ler shofbeebron]
child care centre	la crèche [kresh]
child reduction	la réduction (pour) enfants [la raidookseeyon (poor) onfon]
child's safety seat	le siège-enfant [ler seeyaijonfon]
dummy	la sucette [la soosett]
paddling pool	la pataugeoire [la patojwar]
playground	le terrain de jeux [ler tairand jer]
playmates	les petits copains [ptee kopan]
rubber ring	la bouée [la booai]
toys	les jouets *m* [lai jwai]

Making Friends

What is your name? Comment tu t'appelles? [komon too tapell]
My name is ... Je m'appelle ... [jer mapell]
Where are you from? Tu es d'où? [too ai doo]
I come from ... Je viens de ... [jer veeyan der]
Do you want to play with me? Tu veux jouer avec moi? [too ver jwai avek mwa]

beach
la plage
[la plaj]

castle
le chateau de sable
[lef shato der sabl]

changing room
la cabine
[la kabeen]

sunshade
le parasol
[ler parasol]

ice-cream
la glace
[la glas]

lifeguard
le maître-nageur
[ler metr najuhr]

sailing-boat
le bateau à voiles
[ler bato a vwal]

spade
la pelle
[la pel]

towel
la serviette de bain
[la sairveeyett der ban]

raft
le radeau
[ler rado]

ball
le ballon
[ler balon]

water
l'eau *f*
[lo]

TRAVELLING WITH CHILDREN

baker's
la boulangerie
[la boolonjree]

street
la rue
[la roo]

car
la voiture
[la vwatoor]

police
la police
[la polees]

traffic lights
le feu (de circulation)
[ler feu (der seerkoolaseeyon)]

dog
le chien
[ler sheeyan]

accident
l'accident m
[lakseedon]

bike
le vélo
[ler vailo]

fire-brigade
les pompiers
[lai ponpeeyai]

tram
le tram
[ler tram]

The Essentials

LA BANQUE/LE CHANGE [la bonk/ler shonj]

Where's the nearest ...?
Pardon, Mme/Mlle/M., je cherche ... [pardon madam/madmwazell/mer_syer jer shairsh]

    bank?
    une banque. [oon bonk]

    bureau de change?
    un bureau de change. [an byoorod shonj]

I'd like to change ...
pounds into francs.
Je voudrais changer ... livres sterling en francs. [jvoodrai shonjai ... leevr stairleeng on fron]

I'd like to pay in ...
Je voudrais encaisser ... [jvoodrai onkaisai]

    this eurocheque.
    cet eurochèque. [set_erroshek]

    this traveller's-cheque.
    ce chèque de voyage. [ser shek der vwaeeyaj]

Can I see your cheque card, please?
Votre carte (de chèque), s.v.p. [votr kart (der shek) seel voo plai]

May I see ..., please?
Vous avez ..., s.v.p.? [vooz_avai ... seel voo plai]

    your passport
    votre passeport [votr paspor]

    your identity card
    une pièce d'identité [oon peeyess deedonteetai]

Sign here, please.
Vous signez ici, s.v.p. [voo seenyai eesee seel voo plai]

amount	le montant [ler monton]
bank	la banque [la bonk]
banknote	le billet [ler beeyai]
British pound(s)	livre sterling [leevr stairleeng]
bureau de change	le bureau de change [ler byoorod shonj]
loose/small change	la monnaie [la monai]
to change	changer [shonjai]
cheque card	la carte (de chèque) [la kart (der shek)]
cheque	le chèque [ler shek]
coin	la pièce de monnaie [la peeyess der monai]
credit card	la carte de crédit [la kart der kredee]
currency	la monnaie [la monai]
eurocheque	l'eurochèque *m* [lerroshek]

exchange	le change [ler shonj]
exchange rate	le cours de change [ler koor der shonj]
French franc	le franc français [ler fron fransai]
form	le formulaire [ler formoolair]
money	l'argent *m* [larjon]
to pay out	payer [paiyai]
pin number	le numéro de code [ler noomairod kod]
signature	la signature [la seenyatoor]
traveller's cheque	le chèque de voyage [ler shek der vwaeeyaj]

CUSTOMS / PASSPORT CONTROL
DOUANE/CONTROLE DES PASSEPORTS
[dwan/kontrol dai paspor]

Your passport, please.
Votre passeport, s'il vous plaît.
[votr paspor seel voo plai]

Your passport has expired.
Votre passeport n'est plus valable.
[votr paspor nai ploo valabl]

Have you got a visa?
Vous avez un visa? [vooz avai an veeza]

Can I get a visa here?
Est ce que je peux obtenir un visa ici?
[es_kerj per obterneer oon veeza eesee]

Have you got anything to declare?
Vous n'avez rien à déclarer?
[voo navai reeyann_a daiklarai]

No, I've only got a few presents.
Non, j'ai seulement deux ou trois cadeaux. [non jai suhlmon derzoo trwa kado]

Pull over to the right/the left, please.
Rangez-vous sur la droite, s.v.p.
[ronjai voo soor la drwat seel voo plai]

Open the boot/this case, please.
Ouvrez votre coffre/cette valise, s.v.p.
[oovrai votr kofr/set valeez seel voo plai]

Do I have to pay duty on this?
Il faut le déclarer, ça?
[eel fol daiklarai sa]

Christian name	le prénom [ler prainon]
customs	la douane [la dwan]
date of birth	la date de naissance [la dat der naissonss]
driving licence	le permis de conduire [ler pairmeed kondweer]
duty-free	exempt de droits de douane [aigzon der drwad dwan]
to enter the country	entrer [ontrai]
identity card	la pièce d'identité [la peeyess deedonteetai]
import	l'importation *f* [lanportaseeyon]

to leave the country	quitter le pays [keetai ler payee]
liable to duty	soumis aux droits de douane [soomee o drwad dwan]
maiden name	le nom de jeune fille [ler nond juhn feey]
marital status	la situation de famille [la seetooaseeyond fameey]
married	marié [mareeyai]
single	célibataire [saileebatair]
widower	veuf [vuhf]
widow	veuve [vuhv]
nationality	la nationalité [la naseeyonaleetai]
number plate	la plaque d'immatriculation [la plak deematreekoolaseeyon]
passport control	contrôle des passeports [kontrol dai paspor]
passport	le passeport [ler paspor]
place of birth	le lieu de naissance [ler leeyerd naissanss]
place of residence	le domicile [ler domeeseel]
rabies	la rage [la raj]
surname	le nom de famille [ler nond fameey]
valid	valable [valabl]
visa	le visa [ler veeza]

DOCTOR — LE MÉDECIN [ler maidsan]

At the doctor's — **Chez le médecin** [shail maidsan]

Can you recommend a good ...? — Vous pourriez m'indiquer un bon ... s.v.p.? [voo pooreeyai mandeekai an bon ... seel voo plai]

doctor	médecin [maidsan]
eye specialist	oculiste [okooleest]
gynaecologist	gynécologue [jeenaikolog]
ear, nose and throat specialist	oto-rhino(-laryngologiste) [otoreeno(larangolojeest)]
dermatologist	dermatologue [dairmatolog]
pediatrician	pédiatre [paideeyatr]
neurologist	neurologue [nerrolog]
GP (general practitioner)	généraliste [jainairaleest]
urologist	urologue [oorolog]
dentist	le dentiste [ler donteest]

Where's his surgery? — Où se trouve son cabinet? [oo stroov son kabeenai]

ACCUEIL (Reception)	SALON D'ATTENTE (Waiting room)	CABINET DE CONSULTATION (Surgery)

«Un chat dans la gorge»

We make do with a puny frog, the French, on the other hand, have a spectacular *"cat in their throat"*, when they are a bit hoarse. Makes your eyes water just to think about it!

What's the trouble?	Qu'est-ce qui ne va pas? [kes_keen va pa]
I've got a temperature.	J'ai de la fièvre. [jai dla feeyaivr]
I often feel sick/faint.	J'ai souvent des nausées/vertiges. [jai soovon dai nozai/vairteej]
I fainted.	J'ai eu une syncope. [jai oo oon sankop]
I've got a bad cold.	Je suis très enrhumé. [jer swee traiz_onroomai]
I've got a headache.	J'ai mal à la tête. [jai mal a la tet]
I've got a sore throat.	J'ai mal à la gorge. [jai mal a la gorj]
I've got a cough.	Je tousse beaucoup. [jer toos bokoo]
I've been stung/bitten.	J'ai été piqué/mordu. [jai aitai peekai/mordoo]
I've got diarrhoea./I'm constipated.	J'ai la diarrhée./Je suis constipé. [jai la deeyarai/jer swee konsteepai]
I've hurt myself.	Je me suis fait mal. [jer_mer swee fai mal]
Where does it hurt?	Où est-ce que vous avez mal? [oo es_ker vooz_avai mal]
I've got a pain here.	J'ai mal ici. [jai mal eesee]
I'm a diabetic.	Je suis diabétique. [jer swee deeyabaiteek]
I'm pregnant.	J'attends un enfant/Je suis enceinte. [jaton ann_onfon/jer sweez_onsant]
It's nothing serious.	Il n'y a rien de grave. [eel neeya reeyand grav]
Can you give me/prescribe something for ...?	Vous pouvez me donner/prescire quelque chose contre ..., s.v.p.? [voo poovai mer donai/praiskreer kelker shoze kontr ... seel voo plai]
I usually take...	D'habitude je prends... [dabeetood jer pron]

At the dentist's	**Chez le dentiste** [shail donteest]
I've got (terrible) toothache.	J'ai (très) mal aux dents. [jai (trai) mal_o don]
I've lost a filling.	J'ai perdu un plombage. [jai pairdoo an plonbaj]
I've broken a tooth.	Je me suis cassé une dent. [jerm swee kasai oon don]

71

I'll have to fill it.	Il foudra la plomber. [eel fodra la plonbai]
It'll have to come out.	Il foudra l'enlever [eel fodra lonlvai]
I'd like an injection, please.	Faites-moi une piqûre, s.v.p. [fetmwa oon peekoor seel voo plai]
I don't want an injection.	Ne me faites pas de piqûre, s.v.p. [nerm fet pad peekoor seel voo plai]

In hospital
A l'hôpital [a lopeetal]

How long will I have to stay here?	Combien de temps est-ce que je vais devoir rester ici? [konbeeyand ton es ker jer vai dervwar raistai eesee]
When can I get up?	Quand est-ce que je pourrai me lever? [kont es kerj pooraim lvai]

abdomen	le bas-ventre [ler bavontr]
abscess	l'abcès *m* [labsai]
Aids	le sida [ler seeda]
allergy	l'allergie *f* [lalairjee]
anaesthetic	l'anesthésie *f* [lanaistaizee]
ankle	la cheville [la shveey]
appendix	l'appendice *m* [lapandees]
arm	le bras [ler bra]
artifical limb	la prothèse [la protez]
asthma	l'asthme *m* [lasm]
back	le dos [ler doe]
backache	les douleurs *f* dorsales [lai dooluhr dorsal]
bladder	la vessie [la vaisee]
to bleed	saigner [sainyai]
bleeding	le saignement [sainyermon]
blood	le sang [ler son]
blood clot	l'embolie *f* [lonbolee]
blood pressure	la tension [la tonseeyon]
blood-poisoning	la septicémie [la septeesaimee]
bone	l'os *m* [los]
bowel movement	les selles *f* [lai sel]
brain	le cerveau [ler sairvo]
breast	la poitrine [la pwatreen]
to breathe	respirer [respeerai]
broken	cassé [kasai]
bronchitis	la bronchite [la bronsheet]
bruise	la contusion [la kontoozeeyon]
burn	la brûlure [la brooloor]
bypass (operation)	le by-pass [ler baeepas]
cancer	le cancer [ler konsair]
to catch a cold	prendre froid [prondrer frwa]
cavity	le trou [ler troo]

chest	la poitrine [la pwatreen]
chicken-pox	la varicelle [la vareesel]
circulatory disorder	les troubles *m* de la circulation [lai troobl der la seerkoolaseeyon]
cold	le rhume [ler room]
colic	la colique [la koleek]
concussion	la commotion cérébrale [la komoseeyon sairaibral]
contagious	contagieux/contagieuse [kontajeeyuhr/kontajeeyuhrz]
cough	la toux [la too]
cramp	la crampe [la kronp]
cure	la cure [la koor]
cut	la coupure [la koopoor]
diabetes	le diabète [ler deeyabett]
diarrhoea	la diarrhée [la deeyarai]
difficulty in breathing	les troubles *m* respiratoires [lai troobl respeeratwar]
digestion	la digestion [la deejesteeyon]
dizziness	le vertige [ler vairteej]
to dress	panser [ponsai]
ear	l'oreille *f* [loray]
ear-drum	le tympan [ler tanpon]
examination	l'examen *m* [legzaman]
to extract	tirer [teerai]
eye	l'œil *m* [luh_eey]
face	le visage [ler veezaj]
to faint	s'évanouir [saivanweer]
fever, temperature	la fièvre [la feeyaivr]
filling	le plombage [ler plombaj]
finger	le doigt [ler dwa]
flu	la grippe [la greep]
food-poisoning	l'intoxication *f* alimentaire [lantokseekaseeyon aleemontair]
foot	le pied [ler peeyai]
fracture	la fracture [la fraktoor]
gall-bladder	la vésicule biliaire [la vaizeekool beeleeyair]
German measles	la rubéole [la roobaiol]
gullet	le tube digestif [ler toob deejesteef]
hand	la main [la man]
to have the shivers	avoir le frisson [avwar ler freeson]
head	la tête [la tet]
headache	les maux de tête [lai mod tet]
heart	le cœur [ler kuhr]
heart attack	la crise cardiaque [la kreez kardeeyak], l'infarctus *m* [lanfarktoos]

73

heart defect	la déficience cardiaque [la daifeeseeyons kardeeyak]
heart trouble	les troubles *m* cardiaques [lai troobl kardeeyak]
hernia	la hernie [la airnee]
hip	la hanche [la onsh]
hospital	l'hôpital *m* [lopeetal]
to hurt, to be painful	faire mal [fair mal]
to hurt, to injure	blesser [blessai]
ill, sick	malade [malad]
illness	la maladie [la maladee]
indigestion	les troubles *m* digestifs [lai troobl deejesteef]
infection	l'infection *f* [lanfekseeyon]
inflammation	l'inflammation *f* [lanflamaseeyon]
inflammation of the middle ear	l'otite *f* [loteet]
injection	la piqûre [la peekoor]
injury	la blessure [la blaisoor]
intestines	l'instestin *m* [lantaistan]
jaundice	la jaunisse [la jonees]
jaw	le machoir [mashwar]
joint	l'articulation *f* [larteekoolaseeyon]
kidney stone	le calcul rénal [ler kalkool rainal]
knee	le genou [ler jnoo]
leg	la jambe [la jonb]
lip	la lèvre [la levr]
liver	le foie [ler fwa]
lumbago	le tour de reins [ler toor der ran]
lungs	le poumon [ler poomon]
measles	la rougeole [la roojol]
medical insurance card . . .	la feuille de maladie/de soins [la fuh_eey der maladee/der swan]
menstruation, period	les règles *f* [lai raigl]
migraine	la migraine [la meegrain]
miscarriage	la fausse-couche [la foskoosh]
mouth	la bouche [la boosh]
mumps	les oreillons *m* [laiz_orayon]
muscle	le muscle [ler mooskl]
nausea	la nausée [la nozai]
neck	le cou [ler koo]
nephritis	la néphrite [la naifreet]
nerves	les nerfs *m* [lai nair]
nervous	nerveux [nairver]
nose	le nez [ler nai]
nurse	l'infirmière [lanfeermeeyair]
operation	l'opération *f* [lopairaseeyon]
pacemaker	le stimulateur cardiaque [ler steemoolatuhr kardeeyak]

pain	les douleurs *f* [lai dooluhr]
paralysis	la paralysie [la paraleezee]
poisoning	l'empoisonnement *m* [lonpwazonmon]
polio	la polio(myélite) [la poleeyo(meeyaileet)]
practice, surgery	le cabinet [ler kabeenai]
pregnancy	la grossesse [la grosess]
to prescribe	prescrire [praiskreer]
pulled ligament/muscle	le claquage (musculaire) [ler klakaj (mooskoolair)]
pulse	le pouls [ler poolss]
rheumatism	le rhumatisme [ler roomateesm]
rib	la côte [la kot]
rupture	la hernie [la airnee]
salmonella	les salmonellas *f* [lai zalmonaila]
scan	l'échographie *f* [laikografee]
scar	la cicatrice [la seekatrees]
sexual organs	les organes génitaux [laiz organ jaineeto]
shin	le tibia [ler teebeeya]
shoulder	l'épaule *f* [laipol]
sinusitis	la sinusite [la seenooseet]
skin	la peau [la po]
skull	le crâne [ler kran]
sleeplessness, insomnia	les insomnies *f* [laiz ansomnee]
smallpox	la variole [la vareeyol]
sore throat	le mal de gorge [ler mal der gorj]
specialist	le spécialiste [ler spaiseeyaleest]
spine	la colonne vertebrate [la kolon vairtaibral]
sprained	foulé/e [foolai]
sting	la piqûre [la peekoor]
stomach, tummy	le ventre [ler vontr]
stomach	l'estomac *m* [laistoma]
stomach-ache	les maux *m* d'estomac [lai mo daistoma]
stroke	l'attaque *f* [latak]
sunstroke	l'insolation *f* [lansolaseeyon]
surgeon	le chirurgien/la chirurgienne [sheeroorjeeyan]
surgery *(doctor's)*	le cabinet de consultation [ler kabeenai dai konsooltaseeyon]
surgery *(operation in hospital)*	la chirurgie [la sheeroorjee]
swelling	l'enflure *f* [lonfloor]
swollen	enflé/e [onflai]
to take/pull out	tirer [teerai]

75

tetanus	le tétanos [ler taitanos]
throat	la gorge [gorj]
toe	l'orteil *m* [lortay]
tongue	langue [long]
tonsils	les amygdales *f* [laiz_ameedal]
tooth	la dent [la don]
(to have) toothache	(avoir) mal aux dents [avvar mal o don]
torn ligament	la rupture de tendon [la rooptoor der tondon]
typhoid	la typhoïde [la teefoeed]
ulcer	l'ulcère *m* [loolsair]
unconscious	sans connaissance [son konaissons]
urine	l'urine *f* [looreen]
vaccination	la vaccination [la vakseenaseeyon]
venereal disease	la maladie vénérienne [la maladee vainaireeyen]
virus	le virus [ler veeroos]
to vomit	vomir [vomeer]
waiting room	le salon d'attente [ler salon datont]
ward	la salle [la sal]
wind	le vent [ler von]
wound	la plaie [la plai]
X-ray	faire une radio(graphie) [fair oon radeeyo(grafee)]

LOCAL TRANSPORT — LES TRANSPORTS EN COMMUN [lai tronspor on koman]

Where's the nearest ... bus stop?	Où se trouve ... [oos troov] l'arrêt de bus le plus proche? [laraid boos ler ploo prosh]
tram stop?	l'arrêt de tram le plus proche? [laraid tram ler ploo prosh]
underground station?	la station de métro la plus proche? [la staseeyond maitro la ploo prosh]
Which line goes to ... ?	C'est quelle ligne pour ..., s.v.p.? [sai kel leenyer poor ... seel voo plai]
What time does the bus leave?	A quelle heure part le bus? [a kel uhr par ler boos]
Where do I have to get out/change?	A quel arrêt est-ce que je dois descendre/changer? [a kel_arai ais kerj dwa daisondr/shonjai]
Where can I buy a ticket?	Où est-ce que je peux prendre mon billet? [oo es_kerj per prondr mon beeyai]
To ..., please.	Un billet pour ..., s.v.p. [an beeyai poor ... seel voo plai]

PRACTICAL INFORMATION

bus	le bus [ler boos]
to buy (a ticket)	prendre (son billet) [prondrer (son beeyai)]
departure	le départ [ler daipar]
driver	le conducteur [ler kondooktuhr]
fare	le prix de la course [ler pree dla koors], le prix du billet [ler pree doo beeyai]
to get on	monter (dans le train) [montai (donl tran)]
to get out	descendre [daisondr]
inspector	le contrôleur [ler kontroluhr]
stop	l'arrêt *m* [larai]
street, road	la rue [la roo]
terminus	le terminus [ler tairmeenoos]
ticket	le billet [ler beeyai]
ticket machine	la billetterie [la beeyaitree]
ticket-collector, conductor	le contrôleur [ler kontroluhr]
timetable (for buses/underground/trains)	l'horaire *m* des bus/du métro/des trolleys [lorair dai boos/doo maitro/dai trolai]
tram	le tram [ler tram]
underground	le métro [ler maitro]

LOST-PROPERTY OFFICE — LE BUREAU DES OBJETS TROUVES [ler byooro daiz_objai troovai]

Where's the lost-property office, please?
Où est le bureau des objets trouvés, s.v.p.? [oo_ai ler byooro daiz_objai troovai seel voo plai]

I've lost ...
J'ai perdu ... [jai pairdoo]

I left my handbag on the train.
J'ai oublié mon sac à main dans le train. [jai oobleeai mon sak_a man donl tran]

Please let me know if it's handed in.
Avertissez-moi si on le retrouve. [avairteesaimwa see on ler rtroov]

Here's the address of my hotel.
Voici l' adresse de mon hôtel. [vwasee ladress der mon_otel]

POLICE — LA POLICE [la polees]

Where's the nearest police station, please?
Où est le commissariat de police le plus proche, s.v.p.? [oo ai ler komeesareead polees ler ploo prosh seel voo plai]

I'd like to report an accident.
Je voudrais faire une déclaration d'accident. [jvoodrai fair oon daiklaraseeyon dakseedon]

77

My ... has been stolen.	On m'a volé ... [on ma volai]
handbag	mon sac à main. [mon sak a man]
wallet	mon portefeuille. [mon porterfuheey]
camera	mon appareil-photo. [mon_aparayfoto]
car	ma voiture. [ma vwatoor]
bike	mon vélo. [mon vailo]
My car has been broken into.	On a fracturé la porte de ma voiture. [onn_a fraktoorai la port der ma vwatoor]
I've lost ...	J'ai perdu ... [jai pairdoo]
My son/daughter has gone missing.	Mon fils/Ma fille a disparu. [mon fees/ma feey a deesparoo]
Can you help me, please?	Vous pouvez m'aider, s.v.p.? [voo poovai maidai seel voo plai]
Your name and address, please.	Votre nom et votre adresse, s.v.p.. [votr non ai votr_adress seel voo plai]
Get in touch with the English consulate.	Adressez-vous ou consulat Anglais, s.v.p. [adressai voo o konsoola onglai seel voo plai]

to arrest	arrêter [aretai]
attack, mugging	l'agression *f* [lagreseeyon]
to beat up	rouer de coups [rooaid koo]
car documents	les papiers *m* [lai papeeyai]
car keys	les clés *f* de voiture [lai klaid vwatoor]
car radio	l'autoradio *m* [lotoradeeyo]
cheque	le chèque [ler shek]
cheque card	la carte (de chèque) [la kart (der shek)]
to confiscate	confisquer [konfeeskai]
court	le tribunal [ler treeboonal]
crime	le crime [ler kreem]
drugs	la drogue [la drog]
to harass	importuner [anportoonai]
identity card	la pièce d'identité [la peeyess deedonteetai]
judge	le juge [ler jooj]
key	la clé [la klai]
lawyer	l'avocat/e [lavoka/lavokat]
to lose	perdre [pairdr]
money	l'argent *m* [larjon]
papers, documents	les papiers *m* [lai papeeyai]
passport	le passeport [ler paspor]
pickpocket	le voleur à la tire [ler voluhr a la teer]
police	la police [la polees]
policeman/policewoman	l'agent *m* de police [lajond polees]
prison	la prison [la preezon]
purse	le porte-monnaie [ler portmonai]

rape	le viol [ler veeyol]
to report	faire une déclaration [fair_oon daiklaraseeyon]
theft	le vol [ler vol]
thief	le voleur [ler voluhr]
wallet	le portefeuille [ler porterfuheey]

POST OFFICE — LA POSTE [la post]

Where's ...
    the nearest post office?

    the nearest postbox?

Où se trouve ... [oo stroov]
    le bureau de poste le plus proche?
    [ler byoorod post ler ploo prosh]
    la boîte aux lettres la plus proche?
    [la bwat o letr la ploo prosh]

How much does it cost to send ...
    a letter ...
    a postcard ...
    to ...?

Quel est le tarif d'affranchissement ...
[kel_ai ler tareef dafronsheesmon]
    des lettres ... [dai letr]
    des cartes postales ... [dai kart postal]
    pour ...? [poor...]

I'd like to send this letter ...

    by airmail.
    express.

Je voudrais envoyer cette lettre ...
[jvoodrai onvwaeeyai set letr]
    par avion. [par aveeyon]
    en exprès. [onn_aikspress]

How long does a letter to England take?

Quels sont les délais postaux pour l'Angleterre? [kel son lai dailai posto poor onglertair]

address	l'adresse f [ladress]
addressee	le destinataire [ler daisteenatair]
by airmail	par avion [par_aveeyon]
charge, fee	la taxe [la taks]
collection	la levée [la lervai]
counter, window	le guichet [ler geeshai]
destination	la destination [la daisteenaseeyon]
envelope	l'enveloppe f [lonvlop]
express letter	la lettre exprès [la letr_aikspress]
to fill in	remplir [ronpleer]
form	le formulaire [ler formoolair]
letter	la lettre [la letr]
parcel	le colis [ler kolee]
to post	poster [postai]
post code	le code postal [ler kod postal]
post office	le bureau de poste [ler byoorod post]
postage	le port [ler por]
post-box	la boîte aux lettres [la bwat_o letr]
postcard	la carte postale [la kart postal]
sender	l'expéditeur m [laikspedeetuhr]
stamp	le timbre [ler tanbr]
to stamp	affranchir [afronsheer]
weight	le poids [ler pwa]

TAXI	**LE TAXI** [ler taksee]
Where's the nearest taxi rank?	Pardon, Mme/Mlle/M., vous pourriez m'indiquer la station de taxis la plus proche, s.v.p. [pardon madam/madmwazell/mer_syer voo pooreeyai mandeekai la staseeyon der taksee la ploo prosh seel voo plai]
To the station.	A la gare. [a la gar]
To the ... Hotel.	A l'hôtel ... [a lotel]
To ... Street.	Rue ... [roo]
To ..., please.	A ..., s'il vous plaît [a ... seel voo plai]
How much will it cost to ...?	Il faut compter combien pour aller à ... [eel fo kontai konbeeyan poor_alai a]
Could you stop here, please.	Vous vous arrêtez ici, s.v.p. [voo vooz araitai eesee seel voo plai]
That's for you.	Voilà pour vous. [vwala poor voo]
fare	le prix de la course [ler pree dla koors]
taxi-driver	le chauffeur de taxi [ler shofuhr der taksee]
taxi rank	la station de taxis [la staseeyon der taksee]
tip	le pourboire [ler poorbwar]

TELEPHONING	**TELEPHONER** [tailaifonai]
Can I have a phonecard, please?	Je voudrais une télécarte. [jvoodrai oon tailaikart]
Have you got a ... telephone directory?	Est ce que vous avez un annuaire? [es_ker vooz_avai oon anyooair]
What's the national code for ...?	Quel est l'indicatif de ...? [kel ai landeekateef der]
I'd like to make a call to ...	Je voudrais téléphoner à ..., s.v.p. [jvoodrai tailaifonai a ... seel voo plai]
I'd like to make a reverse charge call.	Je voudrais un numéro en P.C.V. [jvoodrai an noomairo on pai sai vai]
Booth number ...	Cabine numéro ... [kabeen noomairo]
This is ... speaking.	Mme/Mlle/M. ... à l'appareil. [madam/madmwazell/mer_syer ... a laparay]
Hello, who's speaking?	Allô? Qui est à l'appareil? [alo kee ait_a laparay]
Can I speak to Mrs/Miss/Mr ..., please?	Est-ce que je pourrais parler à Mme/Mlle/M. ..., s.v.p.? [es_kerj poorai parlai a mer_syer/madam/madmwazell ... seel voo plai]

> **«Allô!»**
>
> The French always answer the phone with a curt «allô». This is not impolite in any way.

I'm sorry, he's/she's not here.	Je suis désolé/e, il/elle n'est pas là. [jer swee daizolai eel/el nai pa la]
When will he/she be back?	Quand est-ce qu'il/elle sera de retour? [kont_es_keel/el serrad rertoor]
Would you tell him/her that I called?	Dites-lui que j'ai téléphoné. [deet lwee ker jai tailaifonai]

charge	la taxe [la taks]
to dial direct	composer directement [konpozai deerektermon]
to dial	composer le numéro [konposai ler noomairo]
directory enquiries	les renseignements *m* [lai ronsainyermon]
engaged signal	occupé [okoopai]
exchange	le central téléphonique [ler sontral tailaifoneek]
international call	un appel pour l'étranger [ann_apell poor laitronjai]
line	la communication [la komooneekaseeyon]
local call	la communication en ville [la komooneekaseeyon on veel]
long-distance call	la communication interurbaine [la komooneekaseeyon antairoorben]
national code	l'indicatif *m* [landeekateef]
operator	le central téléphonique [ler sontral tailaifoneek]
phone box/booth	la cabine téléphonique [la kabeen tailaifoneek]
(phone) call	le coup de téléphone [ler koo der tailaifon]
phone call (formal)	la communication [la komooneekaseeyon]
phone number	le numéro de téléphone [ler noomairod tailaifon]
phonecard	la télécarte [la tailaikart]
receiver	le combiné [ler konbeenai]
reverse charge call	l'appel *m* en P.C.V. [lapell on pai sai vai]
telephone directory	l'annuaire *m* [lanooair] le Bottin [ler botan]
telephone	le téléphone [ler tailaifon]

Warning!

The following are some of the expressions you should be aware of, so that if they come up in conversation you have some idea of what the person you're talking to might be thinking of you. Be warned: the publishers are not responsible for the consequences of any improper use on your part!

Zut! [zoot]	Damn!
Connard! [konar]	Idiot!
Connasse! [konass]	Silly bitch!
Sale con! [sal kon]	Stupid bastard!
(Espèce de) Salaud! [(espess der) salo]	Bastard!
Quel con! [kel kon]	What an idiot!
(Espèce d') Enculé! [(espess d) onkoolai]	What a tosser, (arsehole)!
Crétin! [kraitan]	Moron!
Ça va pas? [sa va pa]	Are you mad?
(Putain de) Merde! [(pootand) maird]	Shit!
Bordel! [bordell]	Oh shit!
Quelle saloperie! [kel salopree]	What a bloody mess!
C'est dégueulasse! [sai daiguhlas]	That's disgusting!
Je m'en fous! [jmon foo]	I couldn't care less!
Va te faire foutre! [va tfair footr]	(UK) fuck off! (US) fuck you!
Tu m'emmerdes! [too monmaird]	You're getting on my nerves!
Ta gueule! [ta guhl]	Shut your mouth!
Ferme-la! [fairm la]	Shut up!
Casse-toi! [kas twa], Tire-toi! [teer twa]	Clear off! Get lost!

"To have" and "to be", "my" and "your"

avoir [avwar] (to have)		être [etr] (to be)	
j'ai [jai]	I have	je suis [jer swee]	I am
tu as [too a]	you have	tu es [too ai]	you are
il/elle a [eel/el a]	he/she/it has	il/elle est [eel/el ai]	he/she/it is
nous avons [nooz_avon]	we have	nous sommes [noo som]	we are
vous avez [vooz_avai]	you have	vous êtes [vooz_et]	you are
ils/elles ont [eelz/elz_on]	they have	ils/elles sont [eel/el son]	they are

	"my" and "your"			
	singular masculine feminine			plural both genders
singular	mon [mon] ma [ma] ton [ton] ta [ta] son [son] sa [sa]		my your his/her/its	mes [mai] tes [tai] ses [sai]
plural	notre [notr] votre [votr] leur [luhr]		our your(s) their(s)	nos [no] vos [vo] leurs [luhr]

«Moi» and «toi»

Moi [mwa] *(me)* and *toi* [twa] *(you)* are used instead of *je* or *tu* when you want to emphasize them, e.g. (*«Toi aussi»* [twa osee] = "You too").

These words are also used in commands and requests: *«Donnez-moi...»* [donai mwa] ("Give me...(please)").

83

The 1333 most important words

The numbers following the French pronunciation guide in brackets refer to the relevant sections. For tips on pronunciation see page 4.

A

to be able to pouvoir [poovwar], être capable de [etr kapabl der]
about à peu près [a per prai], environ [onveeron]
above au dessus (de) [o dsu (der)]
accident l'accident *m* [lakseedon] → p. 17
accommodation l'hébergement *m* [laibairjermon] → p. 53
to accompany accompagner [akonpanyai]
across à travers [a travair]
activity l'activité *f* [lakteeveetai]
additional supplémentaire [sooplaimontair]
address l'adresse *f* [ladress] → p. 79
addressee le destinataire [ler daisteenatair] → p. 79
adult l'adulte *m/f* [ladoolt]
advance booking la location [la lokaseeyon] → p. 60
to advise conseiller [konsaiyai]
to be afraid (of) craindre [krandr]
afternoon l'après-midi [lapraimeedee] → p. 12
after après [aprai]
again de nouveau [der noovo]
against contre [kontr]
age l'âge *m* [laj] → p. 7
to agree on être d'accord [etr dakor]
aid l'aide *f* [led]
air l'air *m* [lair] → p. 14
alcohol level le taux d'alcoolémie [ler to dalkolaimee] → p. 19
all tous [too], tout [too]
to allow permettre [pairmetr]
to be allowed pouvoir [poovwar]
alone seul [suhl]
along le long de [ler lon der]
already déjà [daija]
also aussi [osee]
to alter modifier [modeefeeyai]
always toujours [toojoor]
ambulance l'ambulance *f* [lonboolonss]
America l'Amerique [lamaireek]
among entre [ontr]
amount le montant [ler monton], la somme [la som] → p. 68
and et [ai]

angry en colère [on kolair]
animal l'animal *m* [laneemal]
annoying fâcheux, -euse [fashuhr, fashuhrz]
to answer répondre [raipondr]
anybody quelqu'un [kelkan]; *(negated)* personne [pairson]
anything quelque chose [kelker shoze]; *(negated)* rien [reeyan]
to apologize s'excuser [sekskyoozai] → p. 7
appetite l'appétit *m* [lapaitee]
appointment le rendez-vous [ler rondaivoo]
area la région [la raijeeyon]
around autour de [otoor der]
arrival l'arrivée [lareevai] → p. 22
to arrive arriver [areevai] → p. 24
as *(cause)* comme [kom]; *(time)* alors [alor]
to ask demander [dmondai]
to assault agresser [agressai]
at à [a]
at once tout de suite [tood sweet]
Atlantic l'Atlantique *m* [latlonteek]
to attack agresser [agressai]
attention! attention! [atonseeyon]
aunt la tante [la tont]
Australia l'Australie *f* [lostralee]
authorities l'administration *f* [ladmeeneestraseeyon]
available disponible [deesponeebl]
average moyen, ne [mwaeeyan, mwaeeyen]
awake réveillé, e [raivaiyai]
awful affreux, -euse [afruhr, afruhrz]

B

baby le bébé [ler baibai] → p. 65
bachelor le célibataire [ler saileebatair]
back de retour [der rertoor]
bad(ly) *adj* mauvais, e [movai, movaiz]; *adv* mal [mal]
band l'orchestre *m* [lorkaistr] → p. 59
bank la banque [la bonk] → p. 68
bar le bar [ler bar] → p. 59
bay la crique [la kreek]
to be être [etr]
beach la plage [la plaj] → p. 61
beautiful beau, belle [bo, bel]

84

because parce que [pars ker]
because of à cause de [a koze der]
to become devenir [dervneer]
bed le lit [ler lee] → p. 54
bee l'abeille *f* [labay]
before avant [avvon]
to begin commencer [komonsai]
beginning le commencement [ler komonsmon]
behind derrière [daireeyair]
to believe croire [krwar]
bell la sonnette [la sonett] → p. 19
to belong to appartenir [aparterneer]
below sous [soo]
bend le virage [ler veeraj] → p. 19
beside à côté de [a kotai der]
besides *(moreover)* d'ailleurs [daieeuhr];
  (in addition) en plus [on ploos]
between entre [ontr]
bicycle le vélo [ler vailo] → p. 15
big grand, e [gron, grond]
bike le vélo [ler vailo] → p. 15
bill la facture [la faktoor] → p. 30
birth la naissance [la naissonss]
birthday l'anniversaire *m* [laneevairsair]
  → p. 10, p. 69
bit, a ~ un peu [an per]
to bite mordre [mordr]
black noir [nwar]
blanket la couverture [la koovairtoor]
blood le sang [ler son] → p. 72
blue bleu [bler]
boat le bateau [ler bato] → p. 62
body le corps [ler kor] → p. 72
to boil bouillir [booeeyeer]
book le livre [ler leevr]
booking la réservation [la raisairvaseeyon]
  → p. 22, p. 26, p. 58
border la frontière [la fronteeyair] → p. 69
boring ennuyeux, -euse [onnweeyer,
  onnweeyerz]
born né, e [nai]
to borrow emprunter [onprontai] → p. 58, p. 62
boss le patron [ler patron]
both tous/toutes les deux [too/toot lai der]
to bother déranger [daironjai]
bottle la bouteille [la bootay]
box office la caisse [la kess] → p. 60
boy le garçon [ler garson]
brake le frein [ler fran] → p. 16
brand la sorte [la sort]
to break casser [kassai]
breakdown la panne [la pan] → p. 16
breakfast petit déjeuner [ptee daijuhnai]
  → p. 33
bright clair, e [klair] → p. 14
to bring apporter [aportai]
brink le bord [ler bor]
broad large [larj]
to broadcast diffuser [deefyoozai]
broken cassé, e [kassai]
brother le frère [ler frair]
brother-in-law le beau-frère [ler bofrair]
building le bâtiment [ler bateemon] → p. 27
bunch of flowers le bouquet [ler bookai]
to burn brûler [broolai]
but mais [mai]
to buy acheter [ashtai] → p. 41
by par [par]
'bye Salut! [saloo]

C

cabin la cabine [la kabeen] → p. 26
to calculate calculer [kalkoolai]
calendar of events le programme des specta-
  cles [ler program dai spektakl] → p. 60
to call appeler [aplai]; **to be called** s'appeler
  [saplai]; **to call on s. o.** rendre visite à qn
  [rondr veezeet_a kelkan] → p. 8
call *(phonecall)* le coup de téléphone
  [ler koo der tailaifon] → p. 81
calm *noun* le repos [ler rerpo]
calm *adj* calme [kalm]
to calm down se calmer [ser kalmai]
camping le camping [ler konpeeng] → p. 57
Canada le Canada [ler kanada]
canal le canal [ler kanal]
to cancel annuler [anoolai]
car la voiture [la vwatyoor] → p. 15
car documents les papiers *m* [lai papeeyai]
  → p. 78
to carry porter [portai]
castle le château [ler shato] → p. 27
cat le chat [ler sha]
cause la raison [la raizon], la cause [la koze]
celebration la fête [la fet]
centre le centre [ler sontr]
certain certain, e [sairtan, sairtenn]
certainly! certainement! [sairtainmon]
to certify attester [atestai]
chair la chaise [la shez]
to change changer [shonjai] → p. 24, p. 76;
  (exchange) échanger [aishonjai]
change la monnaie [la monai] → p. 68
channel le canal [ler kanal]
chapel la chapelle [la shapell] → p. 27
characteristic la caractéristique
  [la karaktaireesteek]
cheap bon marché [bon marshai]
to cheat tromper [tronpai]
to check contrôler [kontrolai]
cheeky éhonté, e [aiontai]
cheerful gai, e [gai]
cheerio! Salut! [saloo]
chemist's *(for prescriptions)* la pharmacie
  [la farmasee] → p. 42; *(for toiletries)* la dro-
  guerie [la drogree] → p. 44
cheque le chèque [ler shek] → p. 68
child l'enfant *m/f* [lonfon] → p. 65
to choose choisir [shwazeer]
Christian name le prénom [ler prainon]
  → p. 69
church l'église *f* [laigleez] → p. 27
cigarette la cigarette [la seegarett] → p. 52
cinema le cinéma [ler seenaima] → p. 60
city centre le centre-ville [ler sontr veel]
  → p. 27
to clean nettoyer [naitwaeeyai] → p. 55
clean propre [propr]
clear clair, e [klair]
clergyman l'ecclésiastique *m*
  [laiklaizeeyasteek]
clever intelligent, e [antaileejon, antaileejont]
cliff la falaise [falaiz]
climate le climat [ler kleema] → p. 14
to climb monter [montai]
clock l'horloge *f* [lorloj]
to close fermer [fairmai]

close proche [prosh]
closed fermé, e [fairmai]
clothing les vêtements *m* pl [lai vetmon]
→ p. 45
coal le charbon [ler sharbon]
coast la côte [la kot] → p. 26
coffee le café [ler kafai] → p. 40
cold froid, e [frwa, frwad] → p. 14
to be cold avoir froid [avwar frwa]
to collect collectionner [kolaikseeyonai]
colour la couleur [la kooluhr]
to come (from) venir (de) [verneer (der)]
to come back revenir [rerverneer]
to come in entrer [ontrai]
common *adj* commun, e [komman, kommoon]
company la société [la soseeyaitai]; *(business)*
l'entreprise *f* [lontrerpreez]
compass la boussole [la boosoll]
compensation la compensation
[la konponsaseeyon]
to complain protester [protaistai]; *(to make a
complaint)* faire une réclamation [fair oon
raiklamaseeyon] → p. 30
complaint la réclamation [la raiklamaseeyon]
→ p. 30
complete complet, complète [konplai, konplet]
concert le concert [ler konsair] → p. 60
condolence(s) les condoléances *f* pl
[lai kondolaionss]
condom le préservatif [ler praizairvateef]
to confirm confirmer [konfeermai]
to confiscate confisquer [konfeeskai] → p. 78
to congratulate féliciter [faileeseetai]
congratulations les félicitations *f* pl
[lai faileeseetaseeyon] → p. 10
connection la correspondance
[la koraispondonss] → p. 23
consulate le consulat [ler konsoola]
contact le contact [ler kontakt]
contents le contenu [ler kontnoo]
to continue continuer [konteenooai]
contraceptive le contraceptif
[ler kontrasepteef]
contract le contrat [ler kontra]
contrary le contraire [ler kontrair]
conversation la conversation
[la konvairsaseeyon]
to cook faire la cuisine [fair la kweezeen]
cool frais, fraîche [frai, fresh]
corner le coin [ler kwan]
corridor le couloir [ler koolwar]
corrupt corrompu, e [koronpoo]
to cost coûter [kootai]
cottage la maison de campagne [la maizon der
konpanyer]
counter *(Bank, Postoffice ...)* le guichet
[ler geeshai] → p. 22, p. 79
country le pays [ler payee]
countryside le paysage [ler payeezaj] → p. 28
couple *(a ~)* une paire [oon pair]; *(partners)*
le couple [ler koopl]
course le cours [ler koor]; *(meal)* le plat
[ler pla] → p. 33
court *(justice)* le tribunal [ler treeboonal]
→ p. 78
cousin le cousin, la cousine [ler koozan, la
koozeen]
credit card la carte de crédit [la kart der
kraidee] → p. 41

to criticize critiquer [kreeteekai]
to cross traverser [travairsai]
crowded plein, e [plan, plen]
to cry pleurer [pluhrai]
culture la culture [la kooltyoor] → p. 27
curious curieux, -euse [kooreeyer, kooreeyerz]
currency la monnaie [la monai] → p. 68
current le courant [ler kooron]
cushion l'oreiller *m* [lorayai]
customs la douane [la dwan] → p. 69
to cut couper [koopai]
cutlery les couverts *m* [lai koovair] → p. 31
to cycle faire du vélo [fair doo vailo] → p. 62

D

to damage endommager [ondomajai], nuire
[nweer]
damages le dédommagement
[ler daidomajmon]
damp humide [oomeed]
to dance danser [donsai] → p. 59
dangerous dangereux, -euse [donjrer, donjrerz]
dark sombre [sonbr]
date la date [la dat] → p. 12, p. 69; *(meeting)*
le rendez-vous [ler rondaivoo] → p. 8
daughter la fille [la feeyer]
day le jour [ler joor] → p. 56
dead mort, e [mor, mort]
deadline la date limite [la dat leemeet]
dear cher, chère [shair]
death la mort [la mor]
to decide décider (de) [daiseedai (der)]
decision la décision [la daiseezeeyon]
to declare déclarer [daiklarai]
to decline refuser [rerfoozai]
deep profond, e [profon, profond]
definite(ly) sans aucun doute [sonz_okun doot]
degree le degré [ler dergrai]
to demand exiger [aigzeejai]
demonstration la manifestation
[la maneefestaseeyon]
denomination la religion [la rerleejeeyon]
dentist le dentiste [ler donteest] → p. 70
department service [sairveess]
departure le départ [ler daipar] → p. 24
deposit l'acompte [akont]
destination la destination [la daisteenaseeyon]
to destroy détruire [daitrweer]
to develop développer [daiverlopai]
to dial composer [konpozai] → p. 81
to die mourir [mooreer]
difference la différence [la deefaironss]
different différent, e [deefairon, deefairont];
differently autrement [otrermon]
difficult difficile [deefeeseel]
direction la direction [la deerekseeyon]
director le directeur [ler deerektuhr]
directory la liste [la leest] → p. 80
dirt la saleté [la saltai]
dirty sale [sal]
disappointed déçu, e [daisoo]
discotheque la discothèque [la deeskotek]
→ p. 59
discount la remise [la rermeez]
to discover découvrir [daikoovrair]
dish le plat [ler pla] → p. 33
distance la distance [la deestonss]

distant éloigné, e [ailwanyai]
district la région [la raijeeyon]
to distrust se méfier de [ser maifeeyai der]
to disturb déranger [daironjai]
disturbance le dérangement [ler daironjmon]
diversion la déviation [la daiveeyaseeyon]
→ p. 20
dizzy pris, e de vertige [pree, preez der vairteej]
to do faire [fair]
doctor médecin [maidsan] → p. 70
documents les papiers m [lai papeeyai] → p. 78
dog le chien [ler sheeyann]
door la porte [la port]
double double [doobl]
to doubt s.th. douter de qc [dootai der]
down(wards) vers le bas [vair ler ba]
to dream rêver [raivai]
drink la boisson [la bwason] → p. 39
to drink boire [bwar] → p. 29
drinking-water l'eau f potable [lo potabl]
→ p. 58
to drive conduire [kondweer]
driving-licence le permis de conduire
[ler pairmeed kondweer] → p. 69
drunk soûl, e [soo, sool]
dry land la terre ferme [la tair fairm] → p. 26
duration la durée [la dyoorai]
during pendant [pondon]
duty le devoir [ler dervwar] → p. 69

E

early tôt [to]
to earn gagner [ganyai]
earth la terre [la tair]
east l'Est m [lest]
easy facile [fasseel]
to eat manger [monjai]
edge le bord [ler bore]
edible comestible [komaisteebl]
education l'éducation f [laidookaseeyon]
effort la peine [la pen]
egg l'œuf m [lerf] → p. 47
either ... or ou ... ou [oo ... oo]
electrician l'électricien m [lailektreeseeyan]
→ p. 45
electrical appliances appareil électroménager
[aparay ailektromainajai]
embassy l'ambassade f [lonbasad]
to embrace embrasser [onbrassai]
emergency brake le signal d'alarme
[ler seenyal dalarm] → p. 24
emergency exit la sortie de secours [la sorteed
serkoor] → p. 23
emergency telephone le téléphone de secours [ler tailaifon der skoor] → p. 20
empty vide [veed]
to end terminer [tairmeenai]
engaged (busy) occupé [okoopai]
engine le moteur [ler motuhr] → p. 16
England Angleterre [onglertair]
English anglais, e [onglai, onglaiz]
the English Channel la Manche [la monsh]
to enjoy jouir de [jweer der]
enough assez [assai]
to enter entrer dans [ontrai don] → p. 69
entertainment le divertissement [ler
deevairteesmon] → p. 59

entire tout [too]
entrance l'entrée f [lontrai]
environment l'environnement m
[lonveeronmon]
Europe l'Europe f [lerrop]
European l'Européen m [lerropayan]
even même [mem]
evening le soir [ler swar]
event l'événement m [laivainmon] → p. 60
every adj chaque [shak]
every time chaque fois [shak fwa]
everything tout [too]
everywhere partout [partoo]
evil méchant, e [maishon, maishont]
exact(ly) exact, e [aigza, aigzakt]
examination l'examen m [laigzaman]
→ p. 73
to examine examiner [aigzameenai]
example l'exemple m [laigzonpl]
except sauf [sof]
exchange le change [ler shonj] → p. 68
to exchange échanger [aishonjai]
exchange rate le taux de change [ler tod
shonj] → p. 69
excursion l'excursion f [lekskoorseeyon]
→ p. 81
excuse l'excuse f [laikskyooz] → p. 7
exhausted épuisé, e [aipweezai]
exhibition l'exposition [laiksposeeseeyon]
exit la sortie [la sortee]
expenses les frais m pl [lai frai]
expensive cher, chère [shair]
to expire expirer [aikspeerai]
to explain expliquer [aikspleekai]
to extend allonger [alonjai]
to extinguish éteindre [aitandr]
to extract tirer [teerai] → p. 73

F

factory l'usine f [loozeen]
fair (noun) la foire [la fwar]
fair (adj) juste [joost]
faith la foi [la fwa]
faithful fidèle [feedell]
to fall tomber [tonbai]
family la famille [la fameey]
far loin [lwan]
farewell adieu [adeeyer] → p. 9
fashion la mode [la mod] → p. 45
fashionable à la mode [a la mod]
fast adj rapide [rapeed]; adv vite [veet]
fat gros, grosse [gro, gross], gras/grasse
[gra/gras]
father le père [ler pair]
fault le défaut [ler daifo]
favourite préféré(e) [praifairai]
fear la peur [la puhr]
to fear craindre [krandr]
fee les frais [lai frai], les honoraires m pl
[laiz_onorair]
feeble faible [febl]
to feel sentir [sonteer]
feeling le sentiment [ler sonteemon]
female féminin, e [faimeenan, faimeeneen]
feminine féminin, e [faimeenan, faimeeneen]
few peu [per]
a few quelques [kelk]

fiancé/fiancée le fiancé [ler feeyonsai]/la fian-
cée [la feeyonsai]
field le champ [ler shon]
to fill in remplir [ronpleer] → p. 79
filling station la station-service
[la staseeyonsairvees] → p. 15
film *(camera)* la pellicule [la peleekyool]
→ p. 60; *(movie)* le film [ler feelm]
finally enfin [onfan]
to find trouver [troovai]
fine *(weather)* beau [bo]; *(well/good)* bien
[beeyan]
fine *(penalty)* amende [amond]
to finish terminer [tairmeenai]
fire le feu [ler fer]
fire alarm l'avertisseur *m* d'incendie
[lavairteesuhr dansondee]
fire brigade les pompiers *m pl* [lai ponpeeyai]
fire extinguisher l'extincteur *m* [laikstanktuhr] → p. 20
firm l'entreprise *f* [lontrerpreez]
first *(~ place)* premier, première [premeeyai/
premeeyair]; *(at first)* d'abord [dabor]
fish le poisson [ler pwasson] → p. 36
flash *(of lightning)* l'éclair *m* [laiklair] → p. 51
flat l'appartement *m* [lapartermon]
flight le vol [ler vol] → p. 22
to flirt draguer [dragai] → p. 8
floor l'étage *m* [laitaj]
to flow couler [koolai]
flower la fleur [la fluhr]
fly la mouche [la moosh]
to fly voler [volai]
to follow suivre [sweevr]
food *(meal)* le repas [ler rpa] → p. 31; *(food-
stuffs)* les denrées *f pl* alimentaires [lai
donrai aleemontair] → p. 29
for pour [poor]; *(because)* car [kar]; *(since)*
depuis [derpwee]
to forbid interdire [antairdeer]
forbidden! interdit, e [antairdee, antairdeet]
foreign étranger, -ère [aitronjai, aitronjair]
foreigner l'étranger *m* [laitronjai], l'étrangère *f*
[laitronjair]
forest la forêt [la forai] → p. 28
to forget oublier [oobleeyai]
to forgive pardonner [pardonai]
fork la fourchette [la foorshett]
form le formulaire [ler formoolair] → p. 69, p. 79
fragile fragile [frajeel]
free libre [leebr]
to freeze avoir très froid [avwar frwa]
French français, e [fronsai, fronsaiz]
frequently fréquemment [fraikamon]
fresh frais, fraîche [frai, fresh]
friend (boy~, girl~) l'ami, e [lamee]
friendly aimable [aimabl]
to be friends être amis [etr_amee]
to frighten effrayer [efrayai]
from de, à partir de [a parteer der]
fruit les fruits *m* [lai frwee] → p. 38
full plein, e [plan, plen]; *(full up)* qui n'a plus
faim [kee na ploo fan]
full board la pension complète [la ponseeyon
konplett] → p. 55
fun l'amusement *m* [lamoozmon]
funny amusant [amoozonn]
furious furieux, -euse [fooreeyuhr, fooreeyuhrz]
furniture le meuble [ler muhbl]
fuse le fusible [ler foozeebl] → p. 20

G

to gain gagner [ganyai]
garage le garage [ler garaj] → p. 16
garden le jardin [ler jardan]
gear *(car)* la vitesse [la veetess] → p. 20
gentleman monsieur [mer_syer]
genuine authentique [otonteek]
Germany l'Allemagne *f* [lalmanyer]
to get recevoir [rerservwar]; *(obtain)* procu-
rer [prokoorai]
to get drunk se soûler [ser soolai]
to get engaged to se fiancer à [ser feeyonsai a]
to get out descendre [daisondr] → p. 25, p. 77
to get to know s. o. connaître q. n. [konetr]
→ p. 6
to get up se lever [ser lervai]
gift le cadeau [ler kaddo]
girl la jeune fille [la juhn feey]
to give donner [donnai]
glad heureux, -euse [uhrer, uhrerz]
gladly volontiers [volonteeyai]
glass le verre [ler vair]
glasses les lunettes *f pl* [lai loonett] → p. 50
gnat le moustique [ler moosteek]
to go aller [alai]
God Dieu [deeyer]
good *adj* bon, bonne [bon, bon]; *adv* bien
[beeyan]
goodbye au revoir [orervwa]
government le gouvernement
[ler goovairnermon]
grandfather le grand-père [ler gronpair]
grandmother la grand-mère [la gronmair]
grandson/granddaughter le petit-fils
[ler pteefeess]
grass la pelouse [la perlooz]
grave la tombe [la tonb]
great grand, e [gron, grond]
green vert [vair]
to greet saluer [salooai] → p. 6
grey gris [gree]
grief le chagrin [ler shagran]
ground le sol [ler sol]
ground-floor le rez-de-chaussée [ler raid
shossai]
group le groupe [ler groop]
guarantee la garantie [la garontee]
guest l'hôte *m* [lot]
guest house la pension de famille
[la ponseeyond fameey] → p. 53
guide le guide (touristique) [ler geed
(tooreesteek)] → p. 28, p. 52
guided tour la visite guidée [la veezeet geedai]
→ p. 28
to be guilty (of) être coupable (de) [etr koopabl
(der)]
guitar la guitare [la geetar]

H

hair les cheveux [lai shver] → p. 48
hairdresser's le salon de coiffure [ler salond
kwafoor] → p. 48
half *adj* demi, e [dmee]; *adv* à demi
[a dmee], à moitié [a mwateeyai]
hall l'entrée [lontrai]

halt! Stop! [stop]
handwriting l'écriture [laikreetyoor]
to happen arriver [areevai]
happy heureux, -euse [uhrer, uhrerz]
to harass importuner [anportoonai] → p. 78
hard dur/e [dyoor]
hardly à peine [a pen]
to harm nuire [nweer]
harmful nuisible [nweezeebl]
to have avoir [avwar]
to have to devoir [dervwar], être obligé, e de [etr_obleejai der]
he il [eel]
head la tête [la tett]
health la santé [la sontai]
healthy en bonne santé [on bon sontai]
to hear entendre [ontondr]
heating le chauffage [ler shofaj] → p. 55
heaven le ciel [ler seeyell]
heavy lourd, e [loor, loord]
height l'altitude *f* [lalteetood]
hello Salut! [saloo]
help l'aide *f* [led]
to help s. o. aider qn [aidai kelkan]
her son [son], sa [sa], ses [sai] → p. 83
here ici [eesee]
high haut, e [o, ot]
to hike faire de la randonnée [fair der la rondonai] → p. 63
hill la colline [la koleen]
to hire louer [looai] → p. 58
his son [son], sa [sa], ses [sai] → p. 83
history l'histoire *f* [leestwar]
to hitchhike faire du stop [fair du stop]
hobby le hobby [ler obbee]
hole le trou [ler troo]
holiday le jour férié [ler joor fereeyai] → p. 13
holidays les vacances *f* pl [lai vakonss], le congé [ler konjai]
holiday home la maison de vacances/de campagne [la maizond vakonss/konpanyer] → p. 56
holy saint, e [san, sant]
home la maison [la maizon]
home-made (fait/e) maison [(fai/fet) maizon] → p. 31
to hope espérer [espairai]
hospital l'hôpital *m* [lopeetal] → p. 74
host/hostess l'hôte *m* [lot]
hot chaud, e [sho, shode] → p. 14
hotel l'hôtel *m* [lotell] → p. 53
hour l'heure *f* [luhr]
hours of business les horaires *m* pl d'ouverture [laiz_orair doovairtoor]
house la maison [la maizon]
household goods les articles ménagers [laiz_arteekl mainajai] → p. 49
how *(question)* comment [komon]; **how much/how many** combien [konbeeyan]
to hug embrasser [onbrassai]
hunger la faim [la fan]
hungry, to be ~ avoir faim [avwar fan]
to hurt faire mal [fair mal] → p. 74
husband le mari [ler maree]
hut la cabane [la kaban]

I

I je [jer]
idea l'idée *f* [leedai]
identity card la pièce d'identité [la peeyess deedonteetai] → p. 69, p. 78
if si [see]
ill malade [malad] → p. 70
illness la maladie [la maladee] → p. 70
immediately tout de suite [tood sweet]
impertinent éhonté, e [ayontai]
impolite impoli, e [anpolee]
import l'importation *f* [lanportaseeyon] → p. 69
important important, e [anporton, anportont]
impossible impossible [anposseebl]
in dans [don]
in front of devant [dvon]
in the morning le matin [ler matan]
in time *adv* à temps [a ton], à l'heure [a luhr]
included compris, e [konpree, konpreez]
indoors à l'intérieur [a lantaireeyuhr]
to inform avertir [avairteer], informer [anformai]
information le renseignement [ler ronsainyermon] → p. 15
inhabitant l'habitant *m* [labeeton]
inn l'hôtel *m* [lotell]
innocent innocent, e [eenosson, eenossont]
to inquire se renseigner [ser ronsainyai]
insect l'insecte *m* [lansekt]
inside à l'intérieur [a lantaireeyuhr]
instead of au lieu de [o leeyer der]
to insult offenser [ofonsai]
insurance l'assurance *f* [lassooronss]
intelligent intelligent, e [antaileejon, antaileejont]
to be interested (in) s'intéresser (à) [santairessai (a)]
international international, e [antairnaseeyonal]
to interrupt interrompre [antaironpr]
interruption le dérangement [ler daironjmon]
introduction la présentation [la praizontaseeyon] → p. 6
to invite inviter [anveetai]
Ireland l'Irlande [leerlond]
island l'île *f* [leel]
isolated seul, e [suhl]
item l'objet *m* [lobjai]

J

jewellery les bijoux *m* [lai beejoo] → p. 49
job la profession [la profeseeyon], l'activité *f* [lakteeveetai], le travail [travaey]
joke la plaisanterie [la plaizontree]
journey le voyage [ler vwaeeyaj], le trajet [ler trajai]
journey home le retour [ler rertoor]
joy la joie [la jwa]
to judge juger [joojai]

K

to keep garder [gardai]
key la clé [la klai] → p. 54, p. 78
kind *(type)* la sorte [la sort]
kind *(nice)* aimable [aimabl]
kindness l'amabilité *f* [lamabeeleetai]
kiss le baiser [ler baizai]
to kiss embrasser [onbrassai]
kitchen la cuisine [la kweezeen]
knife le couteau [ler kooto]
to know *(person, place)* connaître [konetr];
(facts) savoir [savwar]

L

to lack manquer [monkai]
lady la dame [la dam]
lake le lac [ler lak]
land le pays [ler payee]
landlord/landlady le patron, la patronne
[ler patron, la patron] → p. 57
language la langue [la long]
large grand, e [gron, grond]
to last durer [doorai]
last dernier, -ière [dairneeyai, dairneeyair]
late tard [tar]
to be late être en retard [etr_on rertar]
later plus tard [ploo tar]
to laugh rire [reer]
lavatory les W. -C. *m pl* [lai vaisai] → p. 54
lawn la pelouse [la perlooz]
lazy paresseux, -euse [paraisser, paraisserz]
to learn apprendre [aprondr]
to leave partir [parteer]
to leave (for) partir (pour) [parteer (poor)]
left (à) gauche [(a) goshe]
to lend prêter [pretai] → p. 58, p. 62
length la longueur [la longuhr]
less moins [mwan]
to let louer [looai] → p. 17
letter la lettre [la letr] → p. 79
lie le mensonge [ler monsonj]
life la vie [la vee]
lifeboat le canot de sauvetage [ler kanod sovtaj]
→ p. 26
lift l'ascenseur *m* [lasonsuhr]
light *(adj)* leger, -ère [laijai, laijair]
light la lumière [la loomeeyair]
lightning l'éclair *m* [laiklair] → p. 14
to like aimer [aimai]; *(wish)* vouloir [voolwar]
like *(prep)* comme [kom], que [ker]
list la liste [la leest]
to listen (to) écouter [aikootai]
little *(small)* petit, e [ptee, pteet]
little *(a bit)* peu [per]
to live habiter [abeetai]
lock la serrure [la sairoor]
to lock (up) fermer à clé [fairmai aklai]
lonely seul, e [serl]
long long, longue [lon, long]
long-distance call la communication inter-
urbaine [la komooneekaseeyon antairoorben]
→ p. 80
to look regarder [rergardai]
to look after surveiller [survayai]
to look for chercher [shairshai]

to look forward to attendre avec impatience
[atondr avek anpaseeyons]
look out! attention! [atonseeyon]
lorry le camion [ler kameeyon]
to lose perdre [pairdr] → p. 77
to lose one's way se perdre [ser pairdr]
loss la perte [la pairt]
lost perdu [pairdoo]
lost-property office le bureau des objets
trouvés [ler byooro daiz_objai troovai] → p. 77
a lot of beaucoup de [bokoo der]
loud fort, e [for, fort]
loudspeaker le haut-parleur [ler oparluhr]
to love aimer [aimai]
low bas, basse [ba, bas]
low season l'avant-saison *f* [lavonsaizon]
→ p. 55
loyal fidèle [feedell]
luck la chance [la shons]
lucky, to be ~ avoir de la chance [avwar der la
shons]
luggage les bagages *m* [lai bagaj] → p. 22
lunch le déjeuner [ler daijuhnai] → p. 29

M

machine la machine [la masheen]
magazine le magazine [ler magazeen] → p. 52
maiden name le nom de jeune fille [ler nond
juhn feey] → p. 70
mainland la terre ferme [la tair fairm] → p. 26
to make faire [fair]
male masculin, e [maskoolan, maskooleen]
man l'homme [lom]
manager le directeur [ler deerektuhr]
map la carte (géographique) [la kart
(jayografeek)] → p. 52
market le marché [ler marshai] → p. 28, p. 42
to marry se marier [ser mareeyai] → p. 70
mass *(church)* la messe [la mess]
material l'étoffe *f* [laitoff]
maybe peut-être [pert_etr]
me moi [mwa] → p. 29
meal le repas [ler rpa] → p. 29
to mean signifier [seenyeefeeyai]
meat la viande [la veeyond] → p. 34
medicine le médicament [ler maideekamon]
→ p. 43
to meet rencontrer [ronkontrai]
menu la carte [la kart] → p. 29
merry gai, e [gai]
message le message [ler messaj]
middle le milieu [ler meeleeyer]
minus moins [mwan]
minute la minute [la meenoot]
misfortune le malheur [ler maluhr]
Miss mademoiselle [madmwazell]
to miss manquer [monkai]
to be missing manquer [monkai]
mistake l'erreur *f* [lairuhr]
to mistake for confondre [konfondr]
to be mistaken se tromper [ser tronpai]
to misunderstand mal comprendre
[mal konprondr]
mixed mixte [meekst]
moist humide [oomeed]
moment le moment [ler momon], l'instant *m*
[lanston]

90

money l'argent *m* [larjon] → p. 68
month le mois [ler mwa] → p. 13
moon la lune [la loon]
more plus [ploos]
morning le matin [ler matan] → p. 11
mosquito le moustique [ler moosteek]
mother la mère [la mair]
motive le motif [ler moteef]
motor le moteur [ler motuhr] → p. 16
motorbike la moto [la moto] → p. 15
mountain la montagne [la montanyer] → p. 28
to move déménager [daimainajai]
Mr monsieur [mer_syer]
much beaucoup de [bokoo der]
mud la boue [la boo]
to mug agresser [agressai]
museum le musée [ler moozai] → p. 27
music la musique [la moozeek]
my mon [mon], ma [ma], mes [mai] → p. 83

N

naked nu, e [noo]
name le nom [ler non] → p. 6 ,p. 69
to name appeler [aplai]
nation la nation [la naseeyon]
national code l'indicatif *m* [landeekateef]
  → p. 80
nationality la nationalité [la naseeyonaleetai]
  → p. 70
native country le pays natal [ler payee natal]
nature la nature [la natyoor]
naughty méchant, e [maishon, maishont]
nausea la nausée [la nozai] → p. 74
near proche [prosh]
necessary nécessaire [naissaissair]
to need avoir besoin de [avvar berzwan der]
neighbour le voisin [ler vwazan]
nephew le neveu [ler nervuhr]
nervous nerveux, -euse [nairvuhr, nairvuhrz]
  → p. 74
never (ne ...) jamais [(ner ...) jamai]
nevertheless malgré cela [malgrai sla]
new nouveau, nouvel, le [noovo, noovell]
New Zealand la Nouvelle Zélande [la noovell
  zelond]
news la nouvelle [la noovell]
newspaper le journal [ler joornal] → p. 42
next le suivant [ler sweevon], la suivante
  [la sweevont]
next to à côté de [a kotai der]
nice sympathique [sanpateek]
niece la nièce [la neeyess]
night le soir [ler swar], la nuit [la nwee]
  → p. 12
night-club la boîte de nuit [la bwat der nwee]
  → p. 59
no *(adv)* non [non]; *(adj)* aucun, e [okan,
  okoon]
nobody (ne ...) personne [(ner ...) pairson]
noise le bruit [ler brwee]
noisy bruyant, e [brweeyon, brweeyont]
noon midi *m* [meedee]
normal normal, e [normal]
north le Nord [ler nor]
not (ne ...) pas [(ner ...) pa]
nothing (ne ...) rien [(ner ...) reeyan]
now maintenant [mantnon] → p. 12

nowhere nulle part [nool par]
nude nu, e [noo]
number le nombre [ler nonbr], le numéro
  [ler noomairo]
nurse l'infirmière *f* [lanfeermeeyair]

O

object l'objet *m* [lobjai]
occasion l'occasion *f* [lokazeeyon]
occupied occupé, e [okoopai] → p. 25
ocean l'océan *m* [osayon]
of de [der]
of course *adv* naturellement [natoorelmon]
to offend offenser [ofonsai]
to offer offrir [ofreer]
office le bureau [ler byooro]
often souvent [soovon]
oil l'huile *f* [lweel] → p. 21, p. 31, p. 48
old vieux, vieille [veeyer, veeyay]
on sur [soor] → p. 15
once une fois [oon fwa]
one un, une [an, oon]; *(3rd person)* on [on]
only seulement [suhlmon]
open ouvert, e [oovair, oovairt]
to open ouvrir [oovreer]
opening hours les horaires *m pl* d'ouverture
  [laiz_orair doovairtyoor]
opinion l'opinion *f* [lopeenyon]
opportunity l'occasion *f* [lokazeeyon]
opposite *(prep)* en face [on fass]
opposite (to) contraire (à) [kontrair (a)]
or ou [oo]
order la commande [la komond] → p. 29
other autre [otr]
our notre [notr], nos [no] → p. 83
outside à l'extérieur [a laikstereeyuhr], dehors
  [de_or]
oven le four [ler foor]
over au-dessus (de) [o dsu (der)]
overseas outre-mer *m* [ootrermair]
to overtake dépasser [daipassai]
to owe devoir [dervwar]
to own posséder [possaidai]
owner le propriétaire [ler propreeyaitair]

P

to pack faire sa valise [fair sa valeez]
package le petit paquet [ler ptee pakai]
to be painful faire mal [fair mal] → p. 74
painting le tableau [ler tablo]
a pair une paire [oon pair]
papers les papiers *m* [lai papeeyai] → p. 78
parcel le paquet [ler pakai] → p. 79
Pardon? Comment? [komon] → p. 5
parents les parents *m pl* [lai paron]
park le parc [ler park]
to park se garer [ser garai] → p. 16
part la partie [la partee]
party la fête [la fet]
pass *(identity card)* la pièce d'identité
  [la peeyess deedonteetai] → p. 78;
  (mountains) le col [ler kol]
passage le passage [ler pasaj]
passenger le passager/la passagère
  [ler pasajai/la pasajair] → p. 23, p. 26

passing through en transit [on tronzeet]
passport le passeport [ler paspor] → p. 70, p. 78
passport control Contrôle des passeports
[kontrol dai paspor] → p. 69
past le passé [ler pasai]
path le chemin [ler shman]
to pay payer [payai]
payment le paiement [ler paymon]
peace la paix [la pai]
people les gens *m pl* [lai jon]; *(populace)* le
peuple [ler puhpl]
per par [par]
percent pour cent [poorson]
performance *(show)* le spectacle [ler spektakl]
→ p. 60
perhaps peut-être [pert_etr]
permission la permission [la pairmeeseeyon]
to permit permettre [pairmetr]
person la personne [la pairson]
to perspire transpirer [tronspeerai]
petrol l'essence *f* [laissonss] → p. 15
petrol station la station-service
[la staseeyonsairveess] → p. 15
to phone appeler [aperlai], téléphoner
[tailaifonai] → p. 80
photo(graph) la photo [la foto] → p. 51
picture le tableau [ler tablo]
piece la pièce [la peeyess]
pillow l'oreiller *m* [lorayai]; *(cushion)* le
coussin [ler koosan]
pity dommage [domaj]
place le lieu [ler leeyer] → p. 10, la place
[la plass] → p. 70
plane l'avion *m* [laveeyon] → p. 22
plant la plante [la plont]
to play jouer [jooai]
play *(theatre)* la pièce [la peeyess] → p. 60
please s'il vous plaît [seel voo plai] → p. 5
pleased (with) heureux, -euse (de) [uhrer,
uhrerz (der)]
pleasure la joie [la jwa], le plaisir [ler plaizeer]
→ p. 59
plus plus [ploos]
poison le poison [ler pwazon]
poisoning l'empoisonnement *m*
[lonpwazonmon] → p. 75
police la police [la poleess] → p. 78
polite poli, e [polee]
politics la politique [la poleeteek]
poor pauvre [povrer]
port le port [ler por] → p. 25
porter le portier [ler porteeyai] → p. 55
position la situation [la seetooaseeyon],
la position [la pozeeseeyon]
possible possible [poseebl]
to post envoyer par la poste [onvwaeeyai par la
post] → p. 79
post office le bureau de poste [ler byoorod
post] → p. 79
to postpone remettre à plus tard [rermetr_a
ploo tar]
pot la casserole [la kasrol]
pottery la poterie [la potree]
prayer la prière [la preeyair]
to prefer préférer [praifairai]
pregnant enceinte [onsant]
to prescribe prescrire [praiskreer] → p. 71
prescription *(med)* ordonnance [ordononss]
→ p. 42

present le cadeau [ler kado]
to be present être là [etr la], être présent, e
[etr praizon, praizont]
pretty joli, e [jolee]
price le prix [ler pree]
priest le prêtre [ler pretr]
prison la prison [la preezon] → p. 78
prize le prix [ler pree]
probable/probably probable [probabl]/probab-
lement [probablermon]
problem le problème [ler problemm]
profession la profession [la profeseeyon]
programme le programme [ler program]
→ p. 63
prohibited! interdit, e [antairdee, antairdeet]
promise la promesse [la promess]
to pronounce prononcer [prononsai]
proper juste [joost]
protection la protection [la protekseeyon]
pub le bistrot [ler beestro], le pub [ler poob],
le bar[ler ba] → p. 59
public public, -ique [poobleek]
public transport les transports en commun
[lai tronspor on koman] → p. 76
to pull tirer [teerai]
punctual à l'heure [a luhr]
punishment la punition [la pooneeseeyon]
purchase l'achat *m* [lasha]
purse le porte-monnaie [ler portmonai]
to push pousser [poosai]
to put mettre [metr]

Q

quality la qualité [la kaleetai]
question la question [la kesteeyon]
quick/quickly rapide [rapeed]/vite [veet]
quiet(ly) doucement [doosmon], calme [kalm]
quite *(entirely)* tout à fait [toot_a fai]; *(to some
degree)* assez [assai]

R

radio la radio [la radeeyo] → p. 55
railway le chemin de fer [ler shmand fair]
→ p. 24
to rain pleuvoir [plervwar] → p. 14
to ramble la randonnée pédestre [la rondonai
paidestr]
rape le viol [ler veeyol] → p. 79
rare/rarely rare [rar]/rarement [rarmon]
rather plutôt [plooto]
to reach atteindre [atandr]
to read lire [leer]
ready prêt, e [prai, pret]
to realize se rendre compte [ser rondr konpt]
really *adv* vraiment [vraymon]
reason la raison [la raizon]; *(cause)* la cause
[la koze]
receipt le reçu [ler rsoo]
to receive recevoir [rserservwar]
recently l'autre jour [lotrer joor] → p. 12
reception la réception [la raisepseeyon]
→ p. 53
to recognize reconnaître [rerkonetr]
to recommend recommander [rerkomondai]
to record enregistrer [onrjeestrai]

to recover se rétablir [ser raitableer]
red rouge [rooj]
reduction la réduction [la raidookseeyon]
→ p. 24
to refuse refuser [rerfoozai]
region la région [la raijeeyon]
to register enregistrer [onrjeestrai]
relation parent, e [paron, paront]
reluctantly sans plaisir [son plaizeer]
to remain rester [raistai]
to remember se souvenir [ser soovneer]
to remind s. o. of s.th. rappeler qc à qn [raplai kelker shoze a kelkan]
rent le loyer [ler lwaeeyai] → p. 57
to rent louer [looai] → p. 17
repair la réparation [la raiparaseeyon] → p. 16
to repeat répéter [raipaitai]
to replace remplacer [ronplasai]
to reply répondre à [raipondr a]
request la demande [la dermond] → p. 7
reservation la réservation [la raizairvaseeyon]
→ p. 25, 56
residence le domicile [ler domeeseel] → p. 70
responsible compétent, e [konpaiton, konpaitont]
rest le repos [ler rerpo]; *(remainder)* le reste [ler raist]
restaurant le restaurant [ler raistoronn], la brasserie [la brasree] → p. 29
result le résultat [ler raizooltai] → p. 63
return le retour [ler rertoor]
to return revenir [rerverneer]
return journey le retour [ler rertoor]
rich riche [reesh]
right *(correct)* juste [joost]
right le droit [ler drwa]
to be right avoir raison [avvwar raizon]
to ring sonner [sonai]; *(phone)* appeler [aplai], téléphoner [tailaifonai] → p. 80
risk le risque [ler reesk]
river la rivière [la reeveeyair]
road la rue [la roo]
road map la carte routière [la kart rooteeyair]
→ p. 21
rock le rocher [ler roshai]
(roll of) film la pellicule [la peleekyool] → p. 51
room l'espace *f* [lespas], la salle [la sal], la chambre [la shonbr] → p. 53
rotten abîmé, e [abeemai]
round rond, e [ron, rond]
route la route [root]
rubbish les ordures *f* pl [laiz_ordyoor] → p. 57
rule la règle [la regl]
to run courir [kooreer]

S

sad triste [treest]
safe sûr, e [syoor]
safety la sécurité [la saikooreetai]
sale la vente [la vont]
same pareil [paray]
satisfied content, e [konton, kontont]
to save sauver [sovai]
to say dire [deer]
scarcely à peine [a pen]
scenery le paysage [ler paysaj] → p. 28
Scotland l'Écosse [laikoss]

to scream crier [kreeyai]
sea la mer [la mair]
season la saison [la saizon] → p. 13
seat la place [la plass] → p. 28
secluded seul, e [suhl]
second la seconde [la sergond]
secret secret, secrète [serkrai, serkrett]
security la sécurité [la saikyooreetai], la garantie [la garontee]; *(deposit)* la caution [la koseeyon], le gage [ler gaj]
to see voir [vwar]
seldom rarement [rarmon]
self-service shop le libre-service [ler leebrersairvees]
to send envoyer [onvwaeeyai]
sender l'expéditeur *m* [laikspedeetuhr] → p. 79
sentence la phrase [la fraz]
separate séparé, e [saiparai]
serious sérieux, -euse [saireeyer, saireeyerz]
to serve servir [sairveer]
service le service [ler sairvees]; *(religious)* l'office *m* [lofeess] → p. 28, 21
to settle *(a bill)* régler [reglai]
sex le sexe [ler seks]
shade l'ombre *f* [lonbr]; *(colour)* la teinte [la tant]
she elle [el]
ship le bateau [ler bato] → p. 25
shoe la chaussure [la shosyoor] → p. 51
shop le magasin [ler magazan] → p. 41
shore le bord [ler bor], le rivage [ler reevaj]
short court, e [koor, koort]; *(brief)* bref, brève [bref, brev]
shortage le manque [ler monk]
shot le coup (de feu) [ler koo (dfer)]
to shout crier [kreeyai]
to show montrer [montrai]
shut fermé, e [fairmai]
to shut fermer [fairmai]
shy timide [teemeed]
sick malade [malad] → p. 70
side le côté [ler kotai]
sights les curiosités *f* [lai kooreeyoseetai] → p. 27
sightseeing tour of the town/city le tour de ville [ler toor der veel] → p. 27
sign l'indication [andeekaseeyon] → p. 21
to sign signer [seenyai]
signature la signature [la seenyatyoor] → p. 69
silence le silence [ler seelonss]
silent calme [kalm]
since depuis [derpwee]
since *(because)* parce que [pars ker]
to sing chanter [shontai]
single *(unmarried)* célibataire [seleebatair] → p. 70
sister la sœur [la suhr]
sister-in-law la belle-sœur [la belsuhr]
to sit être assis, e [etr asee, aseez]
situation la situation [la seetooaseeyon]
size *(clothing)* la taille [la taeey]; *(shoes)* la pointure [la pwantyoor]
sky le ciel [ler seeyell]
to sleep dormir [dormeer]
slim mince [manss]
slow/slowly lent, e [lon, lont]/ lentement [lontmon]
small petit, e [ptee, pteet]
smell l'odeur *f* [loduhr]

to smell sentir [sonteer]
to smoke fumer [foomai]
smoker le fumeur [ler foomuhr] → p. 23
smooth lisse [leess]
to smuggle faire de la contrebande [fair der la kontrerbond]
snack le casse-croûte [ler kaskroot]
snack-bar le fastfood [ler fastfood]
to snow neiger [naijai]
so donc [donk], comme ça [kom sa]
society la société [la soseeyaitai]
soft mou, molle [moo, mol]
solid dur/e [dyoor]
some quelques [kelker]
somebody quelqu'un [kelkan]
something quelque chose [kelker shoze]
sometimes quelquefois [kelkerfwa] → p. 12
son le fils [ler feess]
song la chanson [la shonson]
soon bientôt [beeyanto] → p. 12
sort la manière [la maneeyair], le genre [ler jonr], la sorte [la sort]
sound le ton [ler ton]
source la source [la soorss]
south le Sud [ler sood]
space l'espace f [lespass]
to speak parler [parlai]
speed la vitesse [la veetess]
to spell épeler [aiplai]
to spend the night passer la nuit [pasai la nwee] → p. 53
spoiled abîmé, e [abeemai]
spoon la cuillère [la kweeyair]
sport le sport [ler spor] → p. 61
spring *(water)* la source [la soorss]; *(season)* le printemps [ler pranton]
square la place [la plass]; *(shape)* carré [karai] → p. 28
staff le personnel [ler pairsonel]
staircase l'escalier m [laiskaleeyai]
stairs l'escalier m [laiskaleeyai]
stamp le timbre [ler tanbr] → p. 79
to stand être debout [etr dboo]
star l'étoile f [laitwal]
to start commencer [komonsai]
to startle effrayer [aifraiyai]
state l'Etat m [laita]
station la gare [la gar] → p. 24
stationer's la papeterie [la papaitree] → p. 52
to stay rester [restai]
to steal voler [volai]
steep raide [red]
still *(adj, calm)* calme [kalm]
still *(adv, yet)* encore [onkor]
to sting piquer [peekai]
stone la pierre [la peeyair]
to stop arrêter [araitai]
stop! Stop! [stop]
stop l'arrêt m [larai] → p. 76
story l'histoire f [leestwar]
stout gros, grosse [gro, gros]
stove le poêle [le pwal]
straight on tout droit [too drwa]
strange bizarre [beezar]
stranger l'inconnu, e [lankonoo]
street la rue [la roo] → p. 21, p. 77
strenuous fatigant, e [fateegon, fateegont]
to study faire des études [fair daiz_aityood]
stupid bête [bet]

style le style [ler steel]
suburb la banlieue [la bonleeyer]
subway le passage souterrain [ler pasaj sootairan]
suddenly soudain [soodann]
sufficient assez [assai]
suitcase la valise [la valeez]
sum la somme [la som]
summit le sommet [ler somai]
sun le soleil [ler solay] → p. 14
sunglasses les lunettes f pl de soleil [lai loonett der solay]
sunny ensoleillé, e [onsolayai] → p. 14
supermarket le supermarché [ler soopairmarshai] → p. 42
supplement le supplément [ler sooplaimon] → p. 25
sure certain, e [sairtan, sairtenn]
surname le nom de famille [ler nond fameey] → p. 70
surprised surpris, e [syoorpree, syoorpreez]
to swap échanger [aishonjai]
to swear jurer [joorai]; *(say bad words)* dire des gros mots [deer dai gro mo]
to sweat transpirer [tronspeerai]
to swim nager [najai] → p. 61
swimmingpool la piscine [la peeseen] → p. 61
Swiss Suisse [sweess]
switch l'interrupteur m [lantairrooptuhr]

T

table la table [la tabl]
to take prendre [prondr]; *(take away)* emporter [onportai]
to take care of surveiller [soorvayai]
to take out tirer [teerai] → p. 73
to take part (in) prendre part (à) [prondr par (a)]
to take place avoir lieu [avwar leeyer]
to take *(train ...)* prendre [prondr] → p. 22, p. 76
take-off le décollage [ler daikolaj] → p. 22
talk la conversation [la konvairsaseeyon]
to talk parler [parlai]
tall grand, e [gron, grond]
taste le goût [ler goo]
to taste goûter [gootai]
taxi le taxi [ler taksee] → p. 80
telephone le téléphone [ler tailaifon] → p. 80
to tell dire [deer]; *(~ a story)* raconter [rakontai]
temperature la température [la tonpairatoor] → p. 14
terrible affreux, -euse [afruhr, afruhrz]
than que [ker]
to thank (sb) remercier (qn) [rermairseeyai (kelkan)] → p. 5
Thank you! Merci! [mairsee] → p. 5
that ce [ser], cet [set], cette [set], ces [sai]
theatre le théâtre [ler tai_atr] → p. 60
theft le vol [ler vol] → p. 79
their leur [luhr] → p. 83
then ensuite [onsweet]; *(at that time)* à l'époque [a laipok]
there là [la]
there is, there are il y a [eel_eeya]
therefore donc [donk]

94

ENGLISH-FRENCH DICTIONARY

they ils [eel], elles [el]
thick gros, grosse [gro, gross]
thin mince [manss]
thing la chose [la shoze]
to think penser [ponsai]
to be thirsty avoir soif [avvar swaf]
this ce [ser], cet [set], cette [set]
those ces [sai]
thought l'idée *f* [leedai]
through à travers [a travair]
thunderstorm l'orage *m* [loraj] → p. 14
ticket le billet [ler beeyai] → p. 24, p. 60, p. 64
ticket office la caisse [la kess] → p. 25, p. 64
till jusqu'à [jooska]
time la fois [la fwa]; *(hour)* l'heure [luhr]
   → p. 11; **at that time** à l'époque [a laipok]
timetable l'horaire *m* [lorair] → p. 25
tip le pourboire [ler poorbwar] → p. 32, p. 80
tired fatigué, e [fateegai]
to à [a]; *(up to)* jusqu'à [jooska]
tobacco le tabac [ler taba] → p. 52
today aujourd'hui [ojoordwee] → p. 12
together ensemble [onsonbl]
toilet les W.-C. *m pl* [lai vaisai] → p. 54
tomb la tombe [la tonb]
tomorrow demain [dman]; **tomorrow
   morning** demain matin [dman matan]
too aussi [osee]
too much trop [tro]
tour la visite [la veezeet] → p. 27
tourist information office l'office *m* de tourisme
   [lofeess der tooreesm], le syndicat d'initiative
   [ler sandeeka deeneeseeyateev]
to tow (away) remorquer [rermorkai] → p. 21
towards vers, en direction de, à [vair, on
   deerekseeyon der, a]
town la ville [la veel]
town centre le centre-ville [ler sontrer veel]
   → p. 27
town hall la mairie [la mairee] → p. 28
town map le plan (de la ville) [ler plon (der la
   veel)] → p. 52
toy le jouet [ler jooai]
traffic la circulation [la seerkoolaseeyon]
train le train [ler tran] → p. 24
to transfer *(money)* virer [veerai]
to translate traduire [tradweer]
to travel voyager [vwaeeyajai]
travel agency l'agence *f* de voyages [lajonss
   der vwaeeyaj] → p. 42
traveller's cheque le chèque de voyage
   [ler shek der vwaeeyaj] → p. 69
tree l'arbre *m* [larbr]
trip l'excursion *f* [lekskoorseeyon] → p. 28
trouble la peine [la pen]
true vrai, e [vrai]
to try essayer [aisayai]
tunnel le tunnel [ler toonell]
twice deux fois [der fwa]
typical (of) typique (de) [teepeek (der)], caractéristique (de) [karaktaireesteek (der)]

U

ugly laid, e [lai, led]
umbrella le parapluie [ler paraplwee] → p. 46
uncertain incertain, e [ansairtann, ansairtenn]
uncle l'oncle *m* [lonkl]

unconscious sans connaissance
   [son konaissons] → p. 76
under sous [soo]
to understand comprendre [konprondr]
unfortunately malheureusement
   [maluhrerzmon]
unfriendly peu aimable [per aimabl]
unhappy malheureux, -euse [maluhrer,
   maluhrerz]
unhealthy malsain, e [malsann, malsenn]
United States Les Etats-Unis [laiz_aitazoonee]
unkind peu aimable [per aimabl]
unknown inconnu, e [ankonoo]
unlucky malheureux, -euse [maluhrer,
   maluhrerz]
until jusqu'à [jooska]
up(wards) vers le haut [vair ler o]
urgent urgent, e [oorjon, oorjont]
us nous [noo]
to use utiliser [ooteeleezai]

V

vacant libre [leebr]
vain vaniteux, -euse [vaneeter]; **in ~** inutile-
   ment [eenooteelmon]
valid valable [valabl] → p. 70
value la valeur [la valuhr]
versus contre [kontr]
very très [trai]
view la vue [la voo] → p. 28; *(opinion)* l'opinion *f* [lopeenyon]
village le village [ler veelaj]
visa le visa [ler veeza] → p. 69
visibility la vue [la voo]
visible visible [veezeebl]
to visit rendre visite à qn [rondr veezeet_a
   kelkan] → p. 8
voice la voix [la vwa]
vote la voix [la vwa]
to vote *(ballot)* voter [votai]
voyage le voyage [ler vwaeeyaj]

W

wages la paie [la pay]
to wait (for) attendre [atondr]
waiter/waitress le garçon/la serveuse
   [ler garson/la sairverz] → p. 32
waiting room le salon d'attente [ler salon
   datont] → p. 76, la salle d'attente [la sal
   datont] → p. 25
to wake réveiller [raivayai]
Wales Pays de Galles [payee der gal]
to walk se promener [ser promnai]
wallet le portefeuille [ler portfuheey] → p. 79
to want vouloir [voolwar], désirer [daizeerai];
   (need) avoir besoin de [avvar berzwan der]
war la guerre [la gair]
warm chaud, e [sho, shode] → p. 14
to warn (of/about) mettre en garde (contre)
   [metr_on gard (kontr)], avertir [avairteer]
to wash laver [lavai]
watch la montre [montr]
to watch regarder [rergardai]
water l'eau *f* [loe] → p. 32, p. 56
way *(manner)* la façon [la fasson]; *(path)* le
   chemin [ler shman]

95

we nous [noo]
weak faible [febl]
to wear porter [portai]
weather le temps [ler ton] → p. 14
wedding le mariage [ler mareeyaj], la noce [la noss]
week la semaine [la smen] → p. 12
weekdays jours ouvrables [joor oovrabl]
to weigh peser [perzai]
weight le poids [ler pwa]
to welcome saluer [salooai] → p. 6
welcome bienvenu, e [beeyanvernoo]
well *adv* bien [beeyan]
west l'ouest *m* [lwest]
wet mouillé, e [mooeeyai] → p. 14
what que [ker]
when quand [kon]
whether si [see]
while pendant que [pondon ker]
white blanc [blon]
whole entier, entière [onteeyai, onteeyair], *(all of it)* le tout [ler too]
wide large [larj]
wife la femme [la fam]
to win gagner [ganyai] → p. 64
to wish vouloir [voolwar], to wish for désirer [daizeerai]
with avec [avek]

without sans [son]
witness le témoin [ler taimwan]
woman la femme [la fam]
wood le bois [ler bwa]
woods la forêt [la forai] → p. 28
word le mot [ler mo]
to work travailler [travaeeyai]; *(function)* fonctionner [fonkseeyonai]
work le travail [ler travaeey]
world le monde [ler mond]
to be worried about se faire du souci pour [ser fair doo soosee poor]
to write écrire [aikreer]
wrong faux, fausse [fo, foss]
to be wrong se tromper [ser tronpai]

Y

year l'année *f* [lanai]
yellow jaune [jone]
you tu [too]; *(yourself)* toi [twa]; *(pl, formal)* vous [voo]
young jeune [juhn]
your ton [ton], ta [ta], tes [tai]; *(pl, formal)* votre [votr], vos [vo] → p. 83
youth hostel l'auberge *f* de jeunesse [lobairj der juhness] → p. 58